ATTILIO STAJANO works
liative care ward of a Brus
an industrial researcher
research programmes on Information Technology at
the European Commission, university professor on
Industrial EU Research for Competitiveness in Bologna and at the
Georgia Institute of Technology in Atlanta, GA, and European
Union Fellow at the University of Pittsburgh, PA. His website is
www.stajano.org.

C000171325

ONLY LOVE REMAINS

LESSONS FROM THE DYING
ON THE MEANING OF LIFE

EUTHANASIA OR PALLIATIVE CARE?

ATTILIO STAJANO

Translated from Italian by Patricia Brigid Garvin

Preface by Marie de Hennezel

CLAIRVIEW

Clairview Books Ltd.,
Russet, Sandy Lane,
West Hoathly,
W. Sussex RH19 4QQ

www.clairviewbooks.com

Published in Great Britain in 2015 by Clairview Books

First published in 2013 under the title *L'amore, sempre: Il senso della vita nel racconto dei malati terminali* by Lindau s.r.l., Torino

© Attilio Stajano 2015
Preface © Carnets Nord/Marie de Hennezel 2014
This translation © Clairview Books 2015

A CIP catalogue record for this book is available from the British Library

Print book ISBN 978 1 905570 77 5
Ebook ISBN 978 1 905570 68 3

Fifty per cent of the author's royalties from this book will be donated to Fondation Privée Soins Palliatifs Clinique de l'Europe
(IBAN BE58068250391379; BIC GKCCBEBB)

Cover by Morgan Creative featuring a photograph © Valiunic
Typeset by DP Photosetting, Neath, West Glamorgan
Printed and bound by 4Edge Ltd., Essex

To Michel Stroobant,
palliative doctor,
teacher, friend, and
pioneer of palliative care in Belgium,
and to all the healthcare staff
he has trained and guided for twenty years.

The author would like to thank his wife, Kathleen, and friends and family members who have read this book in the course of its preparation, offering their encouragement, advice and correcting errors: Martine, Catherine, Saura, Cristina, Angel, Isabelle, Piera, Francesco, Aska and Bruce.

Contents

Preface

What Attilio Stajano and I have in common is the profound, shared conviction that to die peacefully, without suffering and surrounded by love and spirituality, is not an exceptional experience.

I know this because for nine years I worked in the first palliative care unit in France, among people for whom curative medicine no longer held any prospects, but who were still alive and wished to remain so until their last breath. Together with a motivated and competent team, we decided to do everything possible to ensure our terminally ill patients did not suffer, and could die at the proper time with the sense of still being the subjects of their own death. Twenty years ago, I wrote about our pilot scheme in a book called *La Mort intime*,[1] whose preface was written by the then dying president, François Mitterrand. The book spread around the world and acted as a model for the development of palliative care units throughout Europe.

In fact, it was at one of these units in Brussels that Attilio generously offered his services as a volunteer after he retired. Reading his narrative, written with delicacy and feeling, I experienced the same emotions I had felt all those years ago. I rediscovered the lessons that the terminally ill had taught me through their way of being, their sense of humour, their humility and their courage.

Offering daily support to men and women whom medicine can no longer heal, yet can assist in the most dignified and humane manner possible, is no trivial matter in a world that denies death and regards the *time of dying* as a useless, painful and absurd time. Public opinion today widely considers that it is better to limit this time rather than live through it. What is the point in waiting for death when we know that medicine will not be able to heal us? But this way we exclude an incomparable experience. And it is precisely this that we discover when reading Attilio's account. Because the last exchanges with someone who is on the verge of death: the looks, the gestures, the words of love, relief or trust, allow those left behind to experience grief in a completely different way and enrich the rest of their lives. We are no longer the same people we were after assisting a relative or friend on the brink of death. Assisting them transforms us. Why is that? Because we are all mortal, aware that we are visitors on this earth, and that those we love will not always be by our side. And if, on the one hand, this closeness to the death of others is a sword that strikes at the heart of our humanity and hurts us, on the other, it brings us back to what is essential.

Of course, it is not easy to assist people in their last moments in hospitals that have moved away from their vocation of caring for and supporting patients, to become instead economically-oriented technocentric structures. There is a whole movement, one in which I actively participated, that has done its utmost to ensure that the practice of palliative care is firmly established in hospitals and in the medical and medical social services. The aim is to develop a *palliative spirit*, so that wherever death occurs, people are able to conclude their lives with dignity. When, for example, the head of a medical oncology department, or the director of a nursing home for non-autonomous elderly people, has grasped the importance of *not abandoning* the patient for whom there is no longer any prospect of recovery, and when there is a medical team and skilled volunteers like Attilio to talk with people who, in fact, often suffer from being banished behind a screen of lies, or to help relatives remain by the side of the one who is about to leave, then the *time of dying* can be a rewarding time.

Yet, by contrast, when the terminally ill feel they are a burden to others and no longer have a place among the living, they often ask to end their lives. This request for euthanasia conceals anguish and despair.

These days, there is a kind of advocacy of premature death. We talk about *the right to die*, the right to choose our own death, our own chosen moment of freedom and dignity. But where is the freedom in this for fragile and vulnerable people who believe they have become a problem for others? What is this narrow conception of dignity that reduces it to an image we have of ourselves, or one we attribute to another person? Have people who are ravaged by illness or advanced age perhaps lost, in our opinion, their dignity as human beings?

Attilio asks the right questions. Troubling questions. And what particularly struck me in the pages that follow is the personal, humble involvement of this man, who takes his readers by the hand in order to show them the road that all of us will one day take. A road made of separation, sometimes painful but rewarding, a road that opens towards the best part of ourselves.

In spite of their situation, the dying offer us an example of what matters in life. They free themselves from the constraints that have burdened their lives. They become lighter. They help us to live in the present and look towards the future 'with optimism and gratitude', without regretting what has been taken by illness or old age. They show us how important it is to accept our vulnerability and to be able to receive from others.

Reading this book leads to the conviction that we should not miss this experience of assisting a loved one who is close to death. We should not be afraid. We should let our hearts speak; let our intuition guide our actions. We will discover unexpected resources in ourselves: a tenderness, a touch, a readiness to assist that, perhaps, we did not even believe ourselves capable of. In brief, we will emerge from this experience more generous and more human, because on the brink of death it is love that has the last word.

Marie de Hennezel

Introduction

My first encounter with death occurred over fifty years ago when my grandmother Alice died. I had almost finished university and was still living with my parents and my sister. My grandmother was a fat, robust woman, strong-willed, dynamic, intelligent, cheerful, independent and unconventional. She was a very important presence in my life and I loved her dearly. When my grandmother became ill five years before she died, she came to live in our home, where my mother cared for her with a dedication that was exemplary. As the illness took hold, my grandmother gradually gave up the countless activities that had filled her days, and her horizon eventually narrowed to the close family circle and her dream of a princely wedding for my sister. My grandmother died in my mother's arms: she was combing my grandmother's hair in readiness for her visit from the Waldensian pastor, her spiritual companion during her last days.

As a volunteer in the department of palliative care[2] at a Brussels hospital in the years since my retirement, I've come to realize that a peaceful death in an atmosphere of affection and spirituality is not an exceptional experience. Terminally ill patients are accompanied to the end of their lives with their pain relieved in a context of human relationships, respect and dignity.

Palliative care is the new face of medicine; it incorporates scientific and technological progress while acknowledging interpersonal relationships and the integrity of the person in his or her various dimensions: physiological, mental, emotional and spiritual. It is a new form of medical care that goes beyond the concept of the hospital business model, in which machines are run to correspond to a balance sheet, and where quality is synonymous with productivity rather than humanity.

Assisting the dying has led me to reflect upon how the perception of the passage of time is relative for we who believe ourselves healthy and immortal, compared with those who are conscious of the inexorable imminence of their death. The value the terminally ill give to their remaining days helps me to decide how to use my time before it's too late, giving me the chance to come closer to an understanding of the meaning of my life, to be aware of my vulnerability, and to prepare myself with serenity for my own death.

At one time, there was greater familiarity with death, which was part of everyday life due to the high infant mortality rate and the tighter family units that included three or four generations. Today's changing health and social conditions, together with medical advances and the new role of the hospital, have distanced and marginalized death to the point that when a relative of ours is dying we are unable to admit that the illness is terminal. In a vain effort to protect, we seek to hide the truth from our family members without even trying to discover whether or not they wish to be told clearly.

I know that I must die. I know that everyone dies sooner or later, yet it's as though I don't believe it and behave as if I were immortal. Even many doctors behave as if they do not consider death to be the natural and inevitable conclusion to existence. They see death as the failure of their efforts and the defeat of medicine, and so they persist in senseless therapies to the bitter end, even if these only lead to a continuation of suffering.

But does death exist? Perhaps not. Perhaps it is only our reception into another world – a mere transition,[3] but one that frightens us: we are afraid of physical pain and of our loss of status and self-esteem in the terminal phase of life. But this fear should not cause us to behave as though we were dead before we really are.[4] We should establish ourselves definitively in the world before we disappear.[5] The problem is not so much knowing if there is life after death as it is of living before we die,[6] and the technological advances of medicine should not turn the role of therapy into one of adding empty days to a life left without personal relationships, but should instead add life to the days that remain for us to live.

This book is a testimony narrated via stories inspired by my current volunteer activities in a hospital, and by personal encounters with suffering and death. It was also written out of a need to communicate emotions and experiences too intense for me to keep inside, even if in some cases it took many years before these emotions could be expressed and shared.

The names of the healthcare providers are fictional, and I assume all responsibility for the thoughts they express since these have been conceived according to my own personal views. I have learned a great deal from the ward's doctors and nurses, and have been inspired by their humanity, their sensitivity, and the richness of their diversity. Dr Charles does not exist. He is the doctor I would have liked to have been. Similarly, I have introduced other characters, such as Tunç, Émile and Angela, in order to narrate certain episodes of my life.

The names of the patients and their personal circumstances have been altered to avoid revealing the private lives of those who have honoured me with their confidence. However, I did not feel the need to alter the names of my parents, or of certain other people whom I attended until their death, because my relationship with them is too deep to be hidden by a literary fiction. Indeed I feel I have their permission to call them by name and recount their lives without revealing any secret, because when I speak of them I am speaking of myself and nothing is invented; everything is inspired by what is experienced and suffered in the mysterious proximity to death, which in the end means drawing closer to the truth and to eternal life.

My Father

My father, Mario, was born at the end of the 1800s. He was nineteen in 1917 when he was drafted into the *Nizza Cavalleria* regiment after the Battle of Caporetto. Most of his fellow officer cadets on the course did not come back from the Front after the Great War, but my father, who at a young age had already survived an attack of cholera in Naples, had a strong constitution, so that even in the mid-1990s he was still in great shape. He awaited the milestone of his hundredth birthday under the illusion that he would receive a bonus of a million lire from his bank as his legendary friend Claudio had done. Claudio had lived to one hundred and three, and on his hundredth birthday, at a time when inflation had not yet eroded the purchasing power of the lira, had received the fantastic sum of one million. By now, however, a million was no longer a great amount, but to my father, who had lost the sense of the value of money, it was enough to dream of the lucky Signor Bonaventura, who won this amount each week in the stories my father read to me during the post-war years from the illustrated weekly stories published in the *Corriere dei piccoli*.

Dad didn't reach his goal: from the age of ninety-six his energy began to dwindle and he grew frail. He said to me, 'The good Lord's secretary must have misplaced my file.' My mother, too, grew old, and for the two of them to live at their home alone became untenable when she fractured the neck of her femur. While she was in hospital I looked for a convalescent nursing home to accommodate them both. They stayed there for a year, then we brought them back to their home after my sister, Piera, and I had arranged an efficient system of home care, inspired by the way the nursing home was run.

In order to cope with this new situation in their lives, I took a training course for several months on how to assist the elderly and the sick. It represented the first step towards my current role as a hospital volunteer engaged in palliative care.

My father worked in a bank for fifty years, making a good career of which he was very proud. He was a strict, fair man who inspired fear in his employees. At home he had the maid call him *signor direttore* – which gives some idea of how he lived his role. During World War II we lived in Rome, and he travelled by bike to his office in the centre. When he spoke of the climb up via Capolecase, I pictured him as the great cyclist Bartali, climbing the Pordoi Pass in the Giro d'Italia. On Sundays we took a bike trip out to the countryside, riding along the Via Salaria as far as a bridge over the Tiber, before the town of Monterotondo, which had been destroyed by the bombing. I was too little to ride alone, so I sat in a child's seat behind my father. I had to sing all the way to prove I hadn't fallen asleep, and I used to think that pedalling would have been less exhausting. Piera was older and already independent, whereas our mother, insecure on two wheels, got down at every crossroads and crossed over on foot with us teasing her.

During the years of elementary school, my mother was my confidant and refuge from the difficulties and nightmares brought on by catechism lessons. Our parish priest terrorized me with threats of hellfire as a punishment for my sins, and demonized my dear grandmother because she was Lutheran, suggesting I convert her. Even Sistilia our maid was considered an evil presence because she declared she'd joined the Communist Party. Yet, in truth, both my grandmother and Sistilia were kinder and gentler to me than any other female presence around me. Certainly more than Piera, who carried out illicit operations with our shared money, or my mother, who made me practise writing my letters a hundred times.

My father, on the other hand, was a reliable but distant presence who rather scared me, though I knew certain reassuring secrets about him. One of these was a discovery I made when I was seven years old, which, given the nature of our relationship, I never spoke to him about. In 1942, when I was four years old, there was not a lot to eat in Rome and I often went to bed with an empty stomach, and sometimes real hunger. Bread was rationed. There was a dark green card with stamps, and each family was entitled to a certain number of *ciriole* per day, depending on the size of the family nucleus. *Ciriole* are bread rolls that weigh less than 100g, and, as a family of four, we were allowed to buy eight a day. My grandmother often took me to Venanzio's, the baker on via Trebbia, to buy bread. I loved the smell of the baked goods in his shop and I was very fond of Venanzio, who was friendly towards children and one day gave me a still-warm *ciriola* to eat on the spot. My grandmother would then take me to the Villa Borghese, and along the way she taught me many things. For example, she taught me to count, and, later, to carry out the basic operations for numbers up to twenty. So one day at the Parco dei Daini, while using acorns to check my answers, I discovered that eight divided by four does not equal three. Yet I had a *ciriola* in the morning, one at lunch and another at dinner, as did Piera for that matter. 'Fortunately, grandma didn't teach my dad to do division,' I said to myself, and I thought, 'Better not say anything to anyone and risk losing a *ciriola* a day.'

Once, when I was in the second elementary class and my father was checking my exercise book, I realized that he'd mastered dividing whole numbers up to twenty, and perhaps beyond. So it was in his heart that he was unable to do division: for two years, he and my mother had eaten only one bread roll a day to save my sister and I from dying of hunger. This discovery shocked me, but I never said anything to anyone, and certainly not to my dad because I was too shy, too touched, and in any case dad did not encourage verbal communication. I kept this discovery like a treasure in the secret part of me. Meanwhile the Allies had arrived: there was pea soup and white bread.

Dad worked for fifty years in the same bank, then lived in retirement for over thirty more years. This second long period enabled him to overcome the strict austerity that had characterized his life and which had prompted him to impose on me, and perhaps even on Piera, the indisputable authoritarian decisions that had led me to leave home as soon as possible to get away from him. Only after a long and difficult time did I find myself finally free and able to take full possession of my life. Over the years, dad improved like good wine, becoming in extreme old age an affectionate and communicative father and grandfather – attentive, and capable of affection. He left a warm memory of himself and was much loved, forging relationships with the people he spent time with. I once saw him surreptitiously kiss the hand of a nurse's assistant who looked after him in the retirement home. In his last years he learned to discover and wonder at the beauty of creation. For him, old age was not a process of gradual limitation but the culmination of a path[7] in which he reached the fullness of his humanity.

My training for assisting old people who are dying has taught me to try to help those at the end of their days to discover that they can be proud of their lives, and that they have done wonderful, admirable things. So one time when I went to Rome to visit my parents I decided to tell my father about my childhood discovery. Dad was half asleep in a chair; he had lost a little of his lucidity, but distant memories were still stored away. He recalled the bread rationing, the way it had been shared out at home, and how we had all suffered. I thanked him and we cried together.

He also remembered another episode, and we pieced together the details. It concerned his older brother, Uncle Federico, a retired air force colonel. I clearly remember Uncle Federico in full uniform: he looked as if he'd swallowed a broomstick. He also had a sword and I'd wondered how he might put it to use in air battles. Anyway, Uncle Federico had found a doorman in Piazza Istria who sold bread on the black market. My uncle had the money to buy the bread, but would never have dared to shop on the black market – he, a one-time senior officer in the air force who said that 'certain things are not done'! His principles intact, my uncle was nonetheless pragmatic, and so he asked my father to go and buy him ten baguettes, promising to give him one free as commission. So Dad went by bike to Piazza Istria with my uncle's money and brought back the booty on his bike rack. Before he delivered the bread to his brother, he dropped by at home. From the bicycle room — the bikes had to be shouldered up to the fourth floor to keep them safe — came a delicious smell of bread. How could I have resisted? I would have gladly eaten a whole baguette, maybe two, but I thought it more prudent to take a bite from the ends of each of the ten loaves, as that way I could blame it on mice if anyone noticed. But on the contrary, the marks of my small teeth were irrefutable proof of my guilt. My father scolded me severely, but I realized he was crying.

Now this great old man was at the end of his strength and no longer hungry; indeed, he couldn't manage to eat anything. But he was able to be moved by his emotions and to recall memories of suffering, sharing and love. What had kept us apart was gone. We were together, we loved each other, and we forgave each other. I said, 'You've been a good father to me and I thank you for your example in life,' and he replied, 'You're a good son and I love you.' This current of love and forgiveness eased my sadness over his death. It's a part of me and of my honouring his memory.

An Old Acquaintance

Silvie, the woman in bed 553/1, is an old acquaintance. Occupying the other bed in the room is Oda, a woman of about sixty-five who arrived recently and doesn't seem to want to talk about herself, whereas we've got to know Silvie well. She's been receiving treatment in the dialysis department for nine years since a kidney, transplanted six years earlier, had to be removed. She came for dialysis three days a week for over a thousand times. During the three or four hours of dialysis, one of us volunteers used to pass by with beverages and all kinds of other comforting things, as well as the willingness to listen and chat.

Silvie is sixty-five years old, for the last twenty the widow of Pierre, with whom she had two children, André and Yvonne. If I didn't know her date of birth I'd say she was ten years older. For a few years now she has no longer been able to walk and so spends her time in an armchair when she's not in bed. This has led to an increase in her weight and causes her back pain. She used to come to dialysis in a wheelchair, brought by the hospital van that takes patients with reduced mobility back and forth. She retains the elegance of an attractive, well-groomed woman, thanks to the assistance she receives at home from a Polish caregiver. Her blue eyes express the serenity of a woman at peace with herself and with the world. Lately, a number of complications have exacerbated her already serious condition and she can't cope anymore. She requires triple bypass surgery, but the doctors have expressed some reservations: they fear that given her general state of health, the operation cannot be performed safely. They patiently and clearly explained the situation to Silvie in the presence of her family doctor and her younger child, Yvonne, who keeps a close eye on her.

Yvonne has only recently been reunited with her mother after a long period of misunderstanding and difficulties. Her presence is very important to Silvie, also because her son, André, lives in Boston, and apart from a visit to Belgium just once a year, contact is limited to occasional calls to his mother. Now Silvie is faced with the problem of deciding whether to undergo surgery. A meeting with the cardiologist is scheduled for the end of the week. Yvonne is very attached to her mother and would do anything to guarantee her a peaceful end. She fears that the operation might be futile and represent an undue risk, but at the same time she feels torn, and is very apprehensive about the next meeting with the cardiologist. To prepare herself, she has consulted with her mother's family doctor, who has advised against the operation, considering it too risky for Silvie.

Dialysis was recently suspended and, after the first two weeks without it, Silvie's general condition had improved, which gave her the illusion of a possible life without unmitigated dependence on dialysis. Then, a few days ago, Silvie was admitted to the internal medicine ward because of a worsening in the chronic constrictive pericarditis she suffers from, one of the side effects of dialysis. After her assessment on the internal medicine ward, Silvie was transferred to the palliative care ward. Her general condition now seems to be in decline and the cardiologist will visit her tomorrow to tell her that the surgery has been postponed.

When I enter her room she greets me affectionately and says, 'I've been settled here really nicely. If you have time to stay for a moment we can talk more privately than we were ever able to in the dialysis unit. I've got a lot of things to tell you'.

I'm pleased by this reception and sit down in front of her. She is seated in a wheelchair, facing a small table where her breakfast is laid. She leans forward on the arms of her chair so she can be closer to me.

'I don't feel ready to face the challenge of a complicated heart operation. At my next consultation with the cardiologist I'm going to refuse the operation they've proposed. Perhaps my time has come, and in any case, I don't want to face any more ordeals. This is the first time since Pierre died — already twenty years ago — that I see Yvonne serene, and I hope that her trials are over. She's found a partner who is a sweet young man, very sensitive and affectionate. He's called Pierre like my poor husband, and he's a gardener at a garden centre. He came to see me yesterday and brought me a little cyclamen plant. Imagine, Yvonne told me that the first time he invited her to his house he'd strewn the threshold with rose petals the way they do in India or in the Congo to welcome the bride into her new home. I think Pierre will know how to love her, protect her and, hopefully, make her happy. Poor thing! She has the right after all she's been through. But I have to tell you something important about me, Attilio.'

After so many years, this is the first time Silvie has shown such a degree of intimacy. I believe this change in behaviour indicates something very special. Silvie leans in to me still further and I do the same.

'Last night, I woke up. A ray of moonlight lit up the room, and in particular this photograph of Pierre, taken around 1970 when he was in his prime. I went back to sleep and I dreamed of him. He said, "Silvie, you're beautiful and I love you." They're the exact words he said one spring day many years ago. We were sitting in the sun at a countryside café near Braine-l'Alleud, on the way to Waterloo, and were eating slices of wholemeal bread with low-fat cheese and radishes, washed down with a schooner of Geuse beer. Then we took a walk in the meadows and Pierre kissed me. It was the first time I felt loved by a boy whom I loved too. It was the most beautiful day of my life, and last night, in the dream, Pierre said the same words he'd said then. When I woke up I felt very emotional. Last night Françoise was on duty. I knew because she'd changed me. Well, I dared to ring the bell and she came almost immediately. "Here I am, Silvie," she said. "Do you need something?" And I said, "Yes, I need to tell you that I'm happy." Then she hugged me and we cried together.'

Silvie is deeply moved and tells me that she feels Pierre close to her, as if he were inviting her to join him.

'I really think the bypass operation won't be any use to me at all.'

Silvie is tired. She's eaten something and wants to go back to bed. There are only two steps between the chair and the bed, but for this short distance she needs all my help. I hold her up and help her until she is seated on the bed, then I get her to turn by lifting her legs. I arrange the pillows and bedcover. She looks at me with her lovely blue eyes, which now seem dimmed with tears. She gives a ghost of a smile, then her head bends and drops to her left side. She is no longer breathing. I say, 'Silvie, you're beautiful.'

I ring the bell, which brings Denise running. She knows that Silvie is a NTBR[8] patient, which means no resuscitation. She whispers to me, 'She's passed away in peace.'

Denise closes the screen around the bed before Oda realizes what has happened. I close Silvie's eyes and remain there in thought beside her while Denise calls the head nurse, who decides to take Silvie's bed to an unoccupied room.

Silvie's perception of being in contact with Pierre before her death reminds me of my mother's death. My parents lived to a great age, cared for in their own home by my sister, Piera, and with the aid of home help we had organized for the day and night with the assistance of Edgar, a nurse from Ecuador who cared for them competently and with affection. My father Mario died rich in years and at peace with himself and God at the age of ninety-nine, after sixty-nine years of marriage. My mother Anita, who was then ninety-two years old, could not bear the idea of being left alone and took refuge in the illusion that her husband had returned to work and was temporarily absent. A wise geriatrician who was treating her explained to us that our mother took refuge in this wild fiction to protect herself from an intolerable reality and suggested that we support her in this pipe-dream.

My mother died of a heart attack a couple of months after my father. The day before, in my presence and that of my daughter,

Cecilia, she had a vision of her husband calling her to him. She became excited in her bed and cried out lovingly: 'Mario!', stretching out her arms towards a corner of the room. The next day, without saying another word, she died peacefully in the arms of my sister Piera.

Returning to the present after this emotional recollection of my mother's death, I sit beside Oda's bed. She has now realized she is alone in the room. It's the first time that I've stayed for any length of time with her. I see a pretty, petite, but very thin woman, who bears the marks of her suffering. Over an embroidered nightgown she wears an elegant woollen crocheted shawl. There must be someone who thinks of her and cares for her. After a silence whose duration I'm unable to gauge due to my emotional state, Oda says to me, 'They've taken her away. Maybe she felt ill. Or it's for dialysis.'

I decide not to respond immediately and remain quiet next to Oda, who at a certain point turns to me to confide, 'I know where she's gone; I won't see her again. I thought I'd be the first; I even told her that. I'd also like to die like that. Peacefully. Maybe if I heard from Antoine...'

I know that Antoine is Oda's son, but we've never seen him at the hospital. I ask Oda, 'Do you know where your son is? Would you like me to get in touch with him?'

Oda cries, then explains to me that Antoine was twenty years old when his father died. He was still living with his parents and was taking a long time to complete his studies. Meanwhile, various small jobs provided him with enough money to live on and kept him from deciding to put his life in order. Oda could no longer bear seeing this overgrown son around the house and told him to face up to his responsibilities. Antoine left five years after his father's death and nothing more was heard of him. After three years, a postcard with his signature arrived from Santiago, Chile, and a year later there was a second postcard, equally brief, from Garoua, a city in Cameroon. Then, for fifteen further years, nothing more. Oda feels guilty for having thrown him out with the idea that it would shake him up, but also, in truth, so that she could secure her own space in which to rebuild her life. Now she believes she won't be able to close her eyes without at least knowing if he's alive and how he is. Ultimately, he's the only person who could give her the serenity she needs to leave in peace like Silvie.

This is the first time that Oda has talked about herself. I remain with her for a long time and I promise that I will see if something can be done. I ask her to tell me more about Antoine, any information that can guide me in a search that promises to be difficult. Then I ask her who the woman is who has been to visit her in recent days.

'It's Dorothée, one of my neighbours. We've been friends for a long time. She also knew Louis, my husband. She comes to see me every day. She brings me a change of underwear and sits by my bed in silence. She's perhaps the only person I have left in the world. When I was at home we'd often spend the evenings together, talking about the memories of our youth.'

'What's your fondest memory?' I ask.

Oda lights up and says without hesitation, 'My wedding day without a doubt! Louis and I were young and in love. We'd known each other since high school days and we'd always been fond of one another. The day of the wedding we had a party in the country with the two families and twenty or so of our friends. Lunch, dancing, and lots of fun. Then we left for our honeymoon in Normandy. It was very special. I'd never been to France, but later on Louis took me twice to Paris and once to Gordes. Louis was a plumber and earned well. In his spare time he played fullback in a third division football team. He was good, and I often went to watch him on Sundays, even when he played an away match in the province. The first years of marriage were fabulous, but later, the ordeal of doctors began because the children we wanted didn't come.

'Finally Antoine was born and we built our lives around him. At school, when he was fifteen or so, the social worker told me that we over-protected him and that he needed more freedom than we allowed him. Yet to me he seemed content and happy, even though he was always a bit slow in everything except running after girls. He went from one to another without ever really wanting to create a family of his own. It must work better in countries where the mother chooses the bride for her son! Who knows where he is now. Who knows if he's happy. Who knows if he ever thinks of his mother!'

'I'll do everything I can to locate him,' I promise Oda. Then I say goodbye because it's time for the ward meeting. I assure her that I'll be back to visit her again in the following days.

It's the day for the weekly meeting of the volunteer team. The ward's consultant informs us about the state of the patients who've arrived during the week, about the condition of those hospitalized in the previous weeks, and everything else that may help us in our work. All the volunteers are invited and there is always at least one nurse. Oda was admitted five days ago and the consultant explains that she has breast cancer with metastases to the bones and kidneys, and resulting inefficient functioning. She has come from a large teaching hospital where they felt that there was no rationale for starting dialysis and that it was no longer possible to continue cancer treatment since any hope of improvement had been excluded. Oda is not in the last stage of life and our doctors are developing a pain therapy that can ensure a degree of well-being for the time she has left. The discussion of new patients always focuses a great deal on their family situation, and therefore we talk about Oda's lonely state: she has a son who has disappeared and a neighbour who visits diligently. I explain that Oda has expressed a desire to get in touch with Antoine and I'm advised to evaluate the case with Véronique, the social worker.

In the afternoon I go to see Véronique and it is clear to me that she has great experience and an incredible network of professional contacts. She calls a couple of co-workers and tells me that there is the chance of receiving help from the Ministry of Foreign Affairs' social services. She has a contact there too, and wastes no time in phoning while I'm still in her office. She passionately explains Oda's case to her colleague at the ministry, who gives it some thought then suggests she contact the consular services, assuring her that they would immediately explore the possibility of launching a search through the weekly newsletter which is sent to all the record offices. She'll get back to us in a few days.

Before going home, I visit Room 553 on the ward and tell Oda that we are attempting to find a way of getting in touch with Antoine, and that we hope to give her more information in the coming days. Oda can hardly believe that her request has been taken to heart and she thanks me, deeply touched.

'May the good Lord bless you.' Then she adds softly, 'I don't dare to hope, and at the same time I'm almost afraid.'

I stay for a while beside her bed, sitting in silence. Oda tells me about the time when Antoine was five and hid in an empty well in the garden of their home then fell asleep. She recalls the desperate search followed by the immense joy of finding him. I tell her I hope there is the same outcome this time. I wish her good night and take my leave, promising to return soon.

Ten days pass before Véronique calls me and asks me to pass by. Oda's condition has deteriorated due to an increase in renal dysfunction. Time is short. The consulate in Douala has responded to the call from the ministry's social services department and has informed them that Antoine was in touch with them recently to renew his passport. The consulate has sent an address and a phone number, but we don't know whether the number is a dwelling or a workplace. We decide to give it a try, hoping to find someone. It's three in the afternoon and we've checked on the Internet that the local time in Cameroon during this season is the same as in Brussels. International calls cannot be made from Véronique's phone, so we ask the switchboard to link us to the number the consulate has given us. We put the phone on speakerphone so that the two of us can listen, but we decide that Véronique will do the talking. We hear the phone ring three or four times, and then the voice of a young woman with a good English accent says 'Hello'. Véronique asks whether it would be possible to speak to Antoine, saying she's a friend of his mother's in Belgium. The girl at the other end seems to know Antoine, but from the way she speaks, the nature of her relationship with him is not clear. She replies that he should be back around six or eight o'clock. Véronique says she will try again, but also leaves her name and mobile number.

We decide to try again from my home that night. Véronique comes to dinner at my house. As we wait to speak with Antoine, we discuss – also with my wife – how to try to establish a relationship with him. We know very little about Antoine and the conversation might be difficult, but Véronique has many resources and is a great communicator. We're sure she'll be able to cope. It's eight o'clock when we try for the first time. A different person answers from the one we spoke to in the afternoon, another female voice, who tells us in French that Antoine is not there but that we might be able to contact him at another number, which she gives us, saying the numbers one by one. She tells us that Antoine heard someone was looking for him and that he was curious to know who still remembered him. This encourages us to immediately call the other number. We manage to connect after many attempts, and eventually we hear the phone ring and a male voice answers.

'I'm Véronique E. Am I speaking to Mr Antoine D.?'

'Yes, that's me. But I don't think I know you.'

'Actually, we don't know each other,' says Véronique, 'but I know your mother in Brussels. I'm a social worker who's assisting your mother and I felt it was necessary to get in touch with you. Mrs. D. speaks about you with great affection, Antoine, and it seems that her greatest wish right now is to know that you're well, that you're happy, and that maybe now and again you still remember your mother. It's very indiscreet of me to involve myself like this in your intimate affairs, but sometimes circumstances force us not to put questions of etiquette in the way of the relationship between two people who, perhaps without knowing it, are trying to heal old wounds and resolve some unfinished business[9] that's weighing on their hearts.'

Antoine replies, 'If you're saying these things to me it means my mother is dying. I've been making my own decisions for many years now, and with some difficulty I've built a new life. What right do you have to pry into my affairs?'

'I decided to search for you and then to call you because your mother doesn't have much time left and there'd no longer be the possibility to prepare this conversation of ours with all the appropriate delicacy. I know I run the risk of bothering you, or even hurting you, but I want to avoid talking to you when it might be too late. Today you have the chance to decide whether or not to take a step towards your mother and renew a relationship that was broken fifteen years ago. Oda's love for you has not diminished, nor her desire to know that you're happy in your new life. Don't worry about Oda wanting to judge your decisions or encumber your life. She's now beyond any temptation to interfere in your affairs. She just needs a moment's connection with her Antoine so that she can leave in peace and bless him in his personal choices.'

'But at what stage is my mother? How much time does she have left to live? And how much time is there for me to reflect and make a decision?'

'It's difficult to answer in terms of days or weeks. You should know that there's no chance of a recovery and that your mother is being assisted in the final stage of her life by a team that is caring for her well-being and serenity. You are able to offer her the encouragement that would help her to pass tranquilly to the other side. I'm appealing to you to reflect and consider how much peace a gesture of reconciliation and love could offer, and how much sadness you may feel if you don't take this opportunity.'

'Please give me time to think and a number where I can call you. I'll be in touch soon.'

Antoine called two days later and said he was willing to make a short trip to Brussels the following week. The latest analyses indicate the onset of kidney failure. The end seems near. Véronique tells him that it might be too late and suggests that he talk to his mother by phone immediately, giving him the direct phone number for the room where Oda is hospitalized.

Véronique and I are now in Oda's room. We tell her that we've found Antoine and that he will call soon. He's fine, he lives in Cameroon, and he wants to come and see her.

Oda is still able to understand what we say. Tears well up her eyes and run down her emaciated cheeks. She looks at Véronique with gratitude. The telephone rings. Véronique answers, greets Antoine, and tells him that she is at his mother's bedside and that he can now talk to her. She holds the receiver to Oda's ear. Her eyes tell us that she hears her son's voice. She mutters something unintelligible and a small smile spreads over her face as tears continue to trace her cheeks. She hears Antoine as he continues to speak to her. We would like to leave them alone, but Oda is not able to hold the cordless phone in her hand. After a while we hear the busy signal. Oda's eyes are closed. She is breathing slowly then seems to doze off. We remain next to her in silence. The phone rings again. Véronique replies and goes out into the corridor. It's Antoine again. Véronique says that Oda is no longer able to speak, but showed signs of recognizing his voice and is now asleep.

Oda never regained consciousness and died peacefully the following night.

Antoine arrived in Brussels two days later. I went to pick him up at the airport and I accompanied him to the hospital. Oda was lying in her bed in a cold room on the ward, dressed in a tasteful nightgown. A beautician had arranged her hair with a rose in it. Rose petals in various colours were scattered on her white bedcover.

Forgiveness

Igor has just been brought by ambulance to our palliative care ward from the Saint-Pierre hospital. He is seventy-eight years old. He is the owner of a small publishing house which he ran until the onset of his illness, and which for the last three years has been managed by Brigitte, his niece, the daughter of his eldest son, Fred. Igor suffers from particularly intense pain due to prostate and bladder cancer, with metastases to the bone and liver. He is accompanied by his wife, Martha, an elegantly dressed woman who looks younger than her sixty-five years. Igor frequently moans in pain and asks Martha to stay by his side.

Helped by the ambulance staff, two nurses, Rose and Denise, carefully move Igor from the stretcher on to the bed, making every effort to ease his suffering. They arrange several pillows and select and adjust the inclination of the mattress. Igor is very tall and broad-shouldered; he must have been an imposing man, but is now reduced to skin and bone. Dr Charles Malder, the doctor on duty, arrives promptly. Charles is just over forty, and his round, plump, friendly face gives him a reassuring appearance. Igor's wife Martha, the nurses and I leave him alone with Igor. Charles remains in the room for half an hour, then spends a further half hour in his office before going to the nurses' station where he hands in a report and asks for immediate treatment.

He explains to the nurses and to me that the patient is particularly distressed due to two broken ribs and an open bedsore. His general condition is compromised by a heart problem and the after effects of recent surgery for the removal of part of his liver. There are no prospects for the remission of the cancer, now generalized, but the end may not be imminent. Charles tells the nurses that the patient is very ill and at the end of his strength. He is completely lucid and has asked to hasten the end, demanding information regarding the formalities for euthanasia,[10] reserving the right to make a decision soon.

I go back into Igor's room, where Martha has just given him a small blue book, which he is turning over in his hands before beginning to read it with keen interest.

'What are you reading?' I ask him.

'It's one of my books, just printed, which my wife Martha went to fetch from the printing works. A small book, certainly my last, called *Beyond the Mountain*. It's about a visit to Tibet to investigate the mystery of transcendence — a study that has taken me thirty years and allowed me to glimpse an oasis in what initially seemed to be a lifeless desert. I'm happy to be holding the first printed copy of a book that took me a great deal of effort to finish during my last two stays at the Saint-Pierre hospital. I was afraid I wouldn't manage to complete it. It's my twelfth book and the one that's most precious to me. I think that a mother holding her newborn baby for the first time must share a feeling similar to mine at this moment. I've become estranged from some of my offspring, whereas I'm in perfect harmony with others. Some of the books from my youth mean nothing to me anymore and I disown them.'

'Martha,' he then says to his wife in a barely audible voice, 'could you please go as soon as possible and collect a few more copies of this book and bring one to me here in the hospital for Attilio, the volunteer who is assisting us.' Turning back to me, he says, 'I'll write a dedication for you. It won't take you long to read it and, if you want to, you can tell me honestly what you think of it. When I was young and wrote my first book I thought they'd talk about nothing else in all the philosophy journals. Now I no longer nurture those ambitions, nor do I need acknowledgement from the outside world. I've finally come to realize that when I publish a book of mine it's I who change while the world turns on its way regardless.'

'Martha,' he says to his wife, 'could you try and get me a cup of liquorice tea? It's the drink I manage to digest the best. Remember, not too hot and with plenty of sugar.'

I say to her, 'Come with me please. I'll show you where to find it, as well as other things.' I take my leave of Igor and accompany Martha to the family living room where a small kitchen is available for preparing an impromptu meal or for reheating food brought from home for the patients. I notice that when Igor speaks to Martha his voice is weak and unsteady, whereas when he talks to me, he puts a little more energy into the way he expresses himself. My experience suggests that this might say something about their relationship.

Making the herbal tea provides a good opportunity for remaining alone with Martha for a moment and beginning to get to know her. As soon as we leave Igor's room, Martha's eyes fill with tears. In the living room, I suggest she sits down and I offer her chocolate.

I've been taught to put my interlocutors at their ease and to listen to them with discretion and respect. Martha speaks to me without stopping. 'For months he's done nothing but go in and out of hospitals. Each time we come home, he's a little weaker. We got married forty-five years ago. I wasn't even twenty and Igor was strong, well over six foot tall, and played basketball. All the girls were after him, but Igor chose me. We had three children and now there are six grandchildren living all over the world. Through all our difficulties, deep down we've always loved each other, even when life was hard to us. In the morning I'm used to preparing two good cups of coffee as soon as I get up. I'm so used to doing it that now I find myself making two cups even when I'm alone. So I'm left with the extra cup and I start to cry, thinking that soon I'll be alone forever. It's strange, because when Igor was well, I often found him annoying and obsessive – paranoid over his books. I'd really had enough of it. But now I'm not able to accept the idea that his illness is unforgiving. And now he's made up his mind to end it all. Once he wrote a book – totally incomprehensible to me – on the proletarian revolution in an imaginary capitalist country, *The Ant with the*

Flag it was called. He wasn't satisfied with it, so he sent the five thousand copies to be pulped. Now he thinks he can pulp that poor body of his that has betrayed him. He doesn't realize that there are people who love him even in his broken state. I'd like to be with him as long as possible. I still need more time. We both have to ask forgiveness for a hurt we inflicted on each other many years ago. If there is a God, I beg him to give us the opportunity to be reconciled before it's too late. This idea of euthanasia is a betrayal. He blithely removes himself from the field and I'm left with this huge weight. It's not fair; it's not possible! Someone has to help us.'

Martha weeps silently. I hand her a box of paper tissues. I prepare two cups of liquorice tea and offer her one.

'No, thanks,' she says, 'I'd rather have chamomile. My relationship with Igor is not quite that symbiotic!'

She delicately blows her nose and dries her eyes, then says, 'How strange! I've never seen you before today and in five minutes I've told you my life story. My natural defences must have weakened.'

We return to Igor's room with two cups of herbal tea. Nurse Rose is beside the bed. She asks Martha to wait outside a moment and requests me to come in. She has treated the bedsore according to Dr Charles' instructions and is setting up a morphine pump. Igor is also incontinent. Asking for my help, Rose sees to protecting him with great discretion and respect. She then gives him some tablets, and, inviting Martha in, says to Igor, 'Liquorice tea is just what you need right now. You'll see, Igor, the pain will begin to lessen very soon.'

Rose is young; she could be Igor's granddaughter. She treats him with respect and deference. I admire the grace with which she performs such intimate and delicate tasks. I wonder how, at the end of her shift, she is able to turn the page and, when she gets home, embrace her young partner after having lavished care all day on patients whose bodies are devastated by disease. One day I ask her about this, and she explains to me that she has learned to concentrate exclusively on what she is doing – actually, on who she is –

at every moment. She feels that her mission as a nurse is to make the suffering bodies of her patients sacred.

'Is it true that you've written a book?' Rose asks Igor. 'I've never seen the author of a real book up close before. Perhaps I wouldn't understand a thing, but I'd like to leaf through it at least.'

Igor puts his book in Rose's small, skilful hands; she feels its weight and looks at it carefully.

'It smells new,' she says.

'Actually, it's just come from my printing works.' He turns to his wife and says, 'Well, now you'll have to ask Brigitte for another two copies. I'll give one to Rose in exchange for a double dose of morphine.'

'At the most two cups of herbal tea,' Rose says, laughing. 'Dr Malder sets the doses of morphine!'

'Thank you, Rose,' Igor says gratefully and almost flirtatiously. 'You're careful, efficient and kind. I feel I'm in good hands.'

When Rose has finished her work and left the room with a smile, Igor says, 'Martha, I can't go on any longer. This has the air of being a quiet place where I could end my days in peace. I've asked Dr Malder about the procedure for requesting euthanasia. It seems less complicated than you might imagine. Soon I'll stop being a burden. Please ask the notary Van Kaster to pass by tomorrow; I want to have everything sorted out before I give the go-ahead.'

Martha does not restrain her tears. She approaches the bed and rests her head on Igor's hands, wetting them with her tears. I leave discreetly, tip-toeing from the room.

After a couple of hours, Martha leaves the room and goes to the nurses' station where she asks if she can speak to the doctor. Dr Malder is still on the ward and finds time to receive her in his office.

Charles Malder could be her son, but Martha treats him with deference and respect, regarding him as though he were God the Almighty. In spite of this, Martha addresses him with desperate urgency, behaving like someone claiming a sacred right.

'Doctor, we have to prevent the process that Igor wants to start.

He has no right to ask for an action that will end his life. Why doesn't he realize that our children and I would feel abandoned and terribly upset? You're a doctor and you have to treat him or alleviate his pain. You can't offer him death.'

'My dear lady,' Dr Malder replies with courtesy and patience, putting his stethoscope on the table as though divesting himself of his authority, 'my job is to ensure as far as possible the well-being of the patient. I hope that the removal or reduction of the pain may help your husband to rethink his request. I don't think he's insensitive or selfish. The pain he's suffered in recent months has been extremely intense, reaching the limit of what is bearable. These conditions are the only reality he's perceived around him, stronger than any other feeling or any other sentiment. If the other doctors and I succeed in containing his suffering, your husband may take a different attitude. It's his life and he can dispose of it within the limits set by medical ethics and the law. You, madam, together with your children, can do a great deal in these circum-stances. Without using any pressure that could be perceived as oppressive, you can create an atmosphere of serenity and well-being that will let him return to the world of emotions and relationships he has cultivated throughout his life, giving it purpose and meaning.'

Once home, Martha calls their three children, first of all the eldest son Fred, who is a little over forty and lives in London with his wife. She asks him to come as soon as possible, explaining the situation and the role the family can play. She also calls Laura and Thérèse, twins who are also around forty, both married with two and three children respectively. Laura lives in Paris and Thérèse in Dubai. Igor is particularly attached to Francine and Jean, Laura's children. Martha insists that all the family should come to Brussels in the hope of being able to persuade Igor to change his mind.

On the phone to Laura she says, 'Time is short and Igor needs to feel the warmth of the family showing him their love. Among other things, we could persuade him to let himself be assisted up to the end and so avoid a step that I wouldn't know how to find peace with.'

The next day Laura announces her arrival with Francine and Jean. This has given confidence to Martha, and a sense of expectancy to Igor, who in the meantime has begun to feel the beneficial effects of the pain therapy prescribed by the medical team.

He has not yet submitted a formal request for euthanasia, leaving Martha to understand that they will talk about it after Laura's visit. The notary has been summoned as Igor requested. Igor has not told anyone about the terms he has changed in the will he filed long ago at the notary's office. After his death it was discovered that Igor had left a generous bequest to the Foundation for Palliative Care, which meant a second psychologist could be employed part-time for six years.

A visit from the chaplain to the palliative care ward has been announced. Igor has expressed the desire not to see him, whereas he welcomed Stéphanie Déperon, the ward's psychologist, who then spoke separately to Martha.

Stéphanie consults with Charles and tells him that she saw Igor was excited at the idea of seeing his daughter and grandchildren, but was absolutely lacking in strength. Charles requests a blood test, which reveals severe anaemia. A consultation with the other two ward doctors leads to the decision to prescribe a blood transfusion, even though one of the doctors is opposed to this. A treatment of this kind is unusual for a dying patient, but in this case it is justified by the desire for Igor to be fully conscious and in a state of well-being during a visit that is very important to him, and which might lead him towards the decision not to carry out his intentions.

Proposing a transfusion to a patient who is contemplating a request for euthanasia is a particularly delicate and difficult task. There is the risk that it will accelerate the decision to end his suffering. Yet Igor accepts the proposal with natural acquiescence, also due to the delicacy with which Stéphanie and Charles propose the transfusion as a way of giving him a little more energy for the visit from his daughter and beloved grandchildren.

At this point Charles is moderately optimistic. Accepting a blood transfusion is a first step towards accepting life. If the visit takes place in the spirit of their relationship and filial love, Igor's attitude might easily become more favourable towards surrendering himself to the natural rhythms of his final phase of life. Charles has taken this challenge to heart. In principle, he is opposed to euthanasia, but he respects the position taken by patients who make an informed request after the alternative proposed by palliative medicine has, in their case, proved inadequate. The terminally ill are admitted to the ward at the request of their general practitioner, but requests for admission focused on seeking euthanasia are not accepted. In his role as a doctor of palliative medicine, Charles feels he should care for patients by ensuring their greatest welfare in the context of situations that are sometimes extreme. He is aware of the arguments held by those who think that euthanasia should be available within a secular state, and that every person has the right to decide how to die,[11] but he also knows that a law authorizing euthanasia opens a Pandora's box from which new abuses and serious irregularities may emerge.[12]

In the past (and still today in some countries) doctors have sometimes been encouraged to take actions that hasten the end of life beyond any regulatory framework, thus risking prosecution and, at times, ethical drift. Moreover, neither in the Netherlands nor Belgium has legislation on euthanasia led to a reduction in the number of cases of euthanasia practised clandestinely.

In Belgium, a 2002 law[13] has established the right of the terminally ill to take an extreme decision in highly circumscribed situations, when every other avenue has proved impractical.

In the weekly ward meetings, Charles has explained to us that he feels the choice of euthanasia in the name of compassion is to deny that patients, regardless of the degradation of their condition, have an intrinsic, objective, ontological dignity. He lives his role as a doctor in the palliative care ward by accepting his impotence in the face of incurable diseases,[14] and by showing his patients that there are alternatives to euthanasia which, in his view, more deeply respect their dignity, overall well-being, and the freedom[15] of those terminally ill and their loved ones. Each time he wins this battle, he feels he has fulfilled his role as a therapist. True freedom is not what the law confers on doctors by making euthanasia legal under certain conditions, but what doctors give to their patients when they help by creating an environment in which they can choose to give a meaning to their illness and the wait for the end.[16]

In this particular case, Stéphanie has told Charles that the couple need to take a step to solve a problem in their relationship that has been weighing on them for twenty years. Stéphanie does not have to give Charles the details of this hurt that exists between Igor and Martha, which they have separately and confidentially revealed to her. Before it becomes irrevocably impossible to do so, both want to find the courage to offer each other the forgiveness that they have gradually been formulating in their hearts. This step, however, is made difficult by so many years of silence and denial. Time and serenity are needed: two rare and precious resources given Igor's condition.

Laura's visit is announced for Saturday. Charles decides to programme the transfusion for Thursday. Stéphanie has prepared the ground and Charles does not have too much difficulty in gaining Igor's consent for the procedure, explaining the expected benefits and possible risks. Igor absolutely wants to be able to connect once more with his beloved grandchildren, and with his daughter, with whom he shares a particular empathy since with her more than anyone else he has been able to open his heart and reveal the secret of the messages concealed in his books.

He therefore agrees to the transfusion. The risks, which he discussed with Dr Malder, do not frighten him; indeed, they almost make the transfusion more tempting. In fact, Igor is pleased to think that if the transfusion causes severe haemolytic reactions or complications to his immune system, his end will be ensured in the short term without recourse to euthanasia, which he understands would create a problem for Martha.

In an attempt to avoid side effects, the transfusion is spread over two days: Thursday and Friday. Igor is under close observation and Charles ascertains that everything goes as planned. Igor regains some of his strength and waits for the visit with joy and impatience, even though he feels humiliated about letting his grandchildren see him in such a condition, close to an end that he has not fully accepted, yet, paradoxically, would like to accelerate.

The two grandchildren are rather scared at the idea of meeting a grandfather different from the one they knew and loved. Francine is eighteen years old. She considers herself to be the favourite niece and the most loved. She doesn't know that one of Igor's most special gifts is to make each person he is close to feel that they are at the centre of his interest.

She has made herself look especially pretty for this visit, as if she were going to a party with her friends. She knows that her grandfather is proud of her and appreciates her intellectual gifts and also her freshness as a young woman in the flower of her youth. Jean is thirteen years old and a little awkward, like many boys of his age who are discovering the mysterious turmoil of adolescence. His grandfather has often seemed distant and boring, too removed from Jean's world, absolutely and hopelessly old fashioned and hidden behind his books. Francine is upset at seeing her grandfather's condition, the effort it takes him to breathe, his pallor and the extreme thinness of his arms. Old memories come to mind of the times he took her to the park and she had fun with him playing at explorers or going on treasure hunts, and of how, when she was tired, he invited her to the Chalet Robinson[17] to drink a hot chocolate while he told her fascinating, made-up stories. To hide her tears, Francine goes up to him and hugs him, but her tears wet Igor's face, and he feels a great force being transmitted to him, more effective than the blood transfusion that has prepared him for this meeting. After a while, Francine is able to speak, and she whispers to her grandfather: 'Yesterday, I dreamed of you. We were in a boat on a lake surrounded by mist. We no longer knew which way to row and I was afraid we'd never find the shore we'd set off from. Then we heard young people singing and you directed the boat towards the source of these voices, and we found a sunny island populated by children and birds. Perhaps they were the ones who'd been singing.'

'It seems a lovely dream. We'll make up one of our stories about it.'

Francine has broken the ice and Jean is ready in turn to approach his grandfather.

'Grandpa, now that I see you I feel calmer. I'd imagined you with masks and tubes like you see in films. That stuff scares me. I don't understand why my silly sister began to cry. You seem in pretty good shape!'

'I'm fine because I see you here beside me with your mum. Thank you for coming. Who knows what other special plans you had for today. Francine is so pretty it seems as if she's all dressed up to go to a dance.'

'Grandpa,' says Jean, 'it's time you updated your vocabulary. Perhaps in your day or in Mum's, kids used to "go to a dance"!'

Laura and Igor look at each other and smile. The atmosphere relaxes and Igor experiences a moment of serenity. After half an hour, Laura sees that her father is tired and absent, not due to a loss of consciousness, but as though he were engrossed in unexpected and serious thoughts.

'Dad,' she says affectionately, taking his hand in hers, 'perhaps we've tired you out.'

'No, it's not your fault,' Igor replies, 'I sense another visit coming. Please ring the bell; I need to see the nurse.'

After a few minutes, Denise appears. Igor gives her a sign and she understands that his family needs to leave the room. She asks them politely to go to the living room for a moment and asks me to

accompany them there. Igor signals for her to look beneath the
bedcovers, then closes his eyes and falls into a doze. Denise sees
that the area between Igor's legs is stained with blood. She calls the
doctor on duty.

During Laura's visit, Martha has had an appointment with
Stéphanie, the psychologist, in her office. Martha has told her that
Igor is a little better, though perhaps it's only a temporary
improvement. She feels she doesn't want to miss this opportunity
for finding the words to articulate her wish, or rather the need for
them to exchange the mutual pardon that is already in their hearts,
but which they have never known how to express. She is convinced
that this step could bring serenity and peace and help both of them
to live these difficult days in a better way.

Their meeting has lasted for over an hour. Eventually Martha
thinks she has found the words of forgiveness and love that she and
Igor have sought for so many years. As she leaves, she cries as she
hugs Stéphanie and thanks her from the bottom of her heart, which
is now open for a decisive encounter.

The doctor on duty is Dr Dorothée Dewitte, an oncologist in her
fifties who has left the internal medicine ward to devote herself to
palliative care. During the consultation with Charles, Dorothée was
against the transfusion. She has studied Igor's medical records
closely, and now, as she examines him, she realizes that the
bleeding is probably due to the bladder cancer. She believes that
nothing can or should be done except to ensure that Igor does not
suffer. Meanwhile, from an initial state of doziness, Igor is entering
a phase of pre-coma. Dorothée gives the necessary instructions,
then, while Denise administers the prescribed medication, she goes
to the living room in search of Martha and accompanies her to
Igor's room. Before entering the room, Dorothée tells Martha that
perhaps the end is near, but that Igor, although not able to express
himself, might not be totally unconscious and may be comforted by
the sound of her voice. Martha is left alone in the room. She sits
down next to the bed and takes Igor's hand in hers. She sits for a

long time in silence then tenderly begins to caress his forehead. After a little while she takes courage and begins to talk to him of love. She calls him *mon p'tit loup*, the pet name she used when they were twenty. Just to utter it makes her cry.

Sitting beside the bed, she rests her face on his pillow, touching his ear with her lips. She whispers to him that she should have found the words a long time ago to tell him what is in her heart, and that now she feels closer to him than ever before, in a moment of truth where nothing can be hidden any longer. She feels Igor squeeze her hand: he is conscious and she must tell him everything, so that, comforted and serene, he can depart in peace.

Igor remains motionless, but a deep sigh seems to indicate to Martha that he is listening. At least this is what she wants to believe; and, in tears, in the twilit room where Igor is spending his last hours, she finds in her heart ancient words of love, and discovers new ones of reconciliation which she has never before been able to express.

Martha feels Igor's hand quiver between hers and she lowers her head onto his shoulder, continuing to talk to him lovingly for a long time. She is not aware that at a certain point Igor has stopped breathing. He is lying with his eyes and mouth open in an attitude of surrender and serenity.

Denise, making her usual rounds, enters the room. She is immediately aware of the situation. She approaches Martha, puts an arm around her shoulders and says, 'You've accompanied him to the end. Igor has just left us. Let's stay together for a moment.'

Martha trembles when she realizes Igor is dead. She turns to Denise and bursts into tears of release, clasping Denise in her arms. Once she is calm again, she says: 'I want to be the one to close his eyes.'

Martha, encouraged by Denise, accomplishes this powerful gesture of farewell with infinite gentleness. She feels Igor's eyelashes give her one final caress. Martha thinks it is his way of telling her that he has heard, understood and shared her message of forgiveness and love. While she remains absorbed and moved beside the lifeless body of her husband, she hears Fred, their first-born son, talking to me in the hallway. I usher him into Igor's room where Martha welcomes him, holding him to her in a tight embrace.

'Thank you for being here now. Your father died peacefully while I spoke to him of my love. He knew you were coming and was hoping to hold you one last time.'

Fred is dismayed at the idea of having arrived too late and seems inconsolable. Martha understands his state of mind.

'It was good that you told us of your visit. Yesterday your father knew you were coming. I know you'd like to have seen him before the end. On the other hand, it was important for me to be alone with him in the final moment. I spent an intense and emotional time with Igor during the last hours of his life. He passed away at a moment of deep intimacy and sharing. But I also arrived too late. It will remain a sadness that we'll have to bear forever.'

Fred hugs his mother and begins to cry silently in her arms.

They Still Have Something To Tell Us

Monique, an eighty-eight-year-old woman, has been with us for two months. She has beautifully kept white hair, an alert, intense gaze, and shows a deep and sincere interest in the people who come to visit her and in the news that concerns her large family, which in these very days includes the birth of her fourteenth great-grandson. Her end is imminent, but her suffering is mitigated by the skilled care of the team of doctors. Relatives and friends come often to see her, and for these visits she dresses up and puts on perfume and make-up (with the help of the beautician who works for the ward) as if she's receiving guests at her large house in Antwerp. She is still completely lucid, and has established by this point a relationship with many of the health care workers on the ward, as well as with the volunteers who take turns at her bedside. She knows she is close to death, which she awaits calmly, feeling protected by the environment in which she is living.

One day she told me she believed in God and that, years earlier, she'd also practised her religion. She explained to me, 'Now I have a more open spirituality that's less influenced by the Church. Some years ago, when I was still able to travel, I spent a few days in a monastery in the south, across the Alps, where I learned that suffering is not in itself liberating, nor is it the meritorious path that atones for sins and leads to salvation as was preached in the preconciliar era. But it is redeeming if it gives rise to gratitude, friendship and dialogue — if we accept being loved and giving love despite the ravages of old age and illness...' At this point our conversation was interrupted by a phone call from one of her nephews. Out of discretion I left her alone, and when I returned a few minutes later, I found her dozing. We never again had the chance to take up a subject that I would have liked to discuss further; a lesson about the need to seize the moment of an encounter, an opportunity that doesn't come back.

For Palliative Care Day, the French-speaking Belgian radio-television station, RTBF, has asked to visit our hospital; in particular, the oncology, dialysis and palliative care units. The hospital management has granted permission and some patients have enthusiastically embraced the opportunity to announce that, in actual fact, they are still alive and still have something to tell us. The journalist sent to the hospital is a well-established figure on Belgian television whom we'll call Susi.

The first person to be interviewed on the palliative care ward is Monique. Susi records a conversation that will then be transmitted on the radio.

Monique says, 'It's hard to let go of life. But two weeks ago I was sure I'd reached the end and I wasn't afraid. I had no idea what palliative care was when I was admitted to this ward. They've helped me in an extraordinary way and I have no words to describe the competence, kindness and friendliness I've received. I've found the conditions for reflecting on my life, and, looking back over it all, I feel a sense of contentment and happiness.'

Many of the health professionals and their families listening to this radio interview had tears in their eyes on hearing this sincere declaration of gratitude. A few days later, I had the chance to thank her and talk to her again. Monique died peacefully a week after the interview while two of her sons were with me at her bedside. She went to find the certainties that she feared she'd lost.

I accompany the journalist on her tour of the wards. Susi has to meet Mireille, who is on the palliative care floor for pain therapy. She is forty years old and suffers from Lou Gehrig's disease: amyotrophic lateral sclerosis. Mireille is so young that she seems out of place in this ward. She has beautiful black hair, the skin of her face is smooth and without wrinkles, and her gaze is alive and penetrating. She is attractive and, at first sight, one doesn't realize the seriousness of her condition. Mireille lives with Marco and has an eleven-year-old son, Thomas. Mireille is unfortunately part of that ten per cent of patients for whom pain therapy fails to relieve all suffering. She has been from one hospital to another without finding relief, becoming a patient whom, in the end, the hospital wants to get rid of. She feels uncomfortable in the palliative care ward, for the most part surrounded by very elderly patients who are near their end, with bodies often ravaged by illness. There will be no reprieve for Mireille from the sclerosis, and she knows that it will continue to make her suffer for many years while her general condition gradually deteriorates. She is torn between the desire to seek death and anguish over abandoning Thomas, who is so young, fragile and vulnerable. Marco is a successful architect whose professional life is compromised by the space Mireille's sclerosis is taking up, bringing him to a state of exhaustion bordering on burn-out. Mireille sees him as resigned and distant, 'as if he were made of wood', and, in her view, inadequate to offer Thomas the kind of relationship that ought to compensate for the absence of his mother. Mireille deludes herself that soon she'll be able to go home, and she'd like to find the strength to separate from Marco, whom she accuses of an absolute lack of human warmth and vital energy.

Mireille asks Susi, the journalist from the RTBF, to sit on her bed. Gripping her wrist, she speaks with sincerity.

'I'd like to feel free to ask for euthanasia. It would be better for me and perhaps for everyone. Yes, even for Thomas, because basically I'm no longer able to be close to him, or help him grow up, or maybe even to love him. This disease is taking hold of me. I feel continuously overwhelmed by a process of degeneration in my motor skills, in the ability to express myself, feed myself and breathe. The pain lives in me and it's dehumanizing me. I always feel like crying. It seems to me that the whole world is against me. In the last months they've moved me from one hospital to another just so I could witness their inability to help me. Here they treat me better, but even they are unable to relieve my constant pain. At least the other patients know they're close to death, whereas I'm facing an undefined path of suffering and decline. How can I be a mother to my Thomas? If I were a bit better, even just a little bit, I could go home and take up my life again. I'd leave Marco and I'd feel myself alive again. But I'm too weak to do it, and so I'm trapped with no way out. Perhaps I'm not letting myself get better because then I'd have to take the step I lack the courage for, but which is absolutely necessary. I've been told that David Niven suffered from my disease. Maybe his artistic passion helped him to live despite everything. I feel crushed and almost beaten. I say 'almost' because basically I still hold on to an absurd hope that prevents me from asking for euthanasia: the idea of seeing Thomas in high school, maybe university. I'm not saying grandchildren, but at least... In these last days I had one single moment of peace when I saw Thomas smile, fascinated by the conjuring tricks performed by the volunteer who's here with you and who often keeps me company. He was present during one of Thomas's after school visits. He performed magic tricks with cards that have left us open-mouthed, and for a moment the only thing I saw was my son's astonished smile, for once distracted from the sight of my disease.'

Mireille cries and covers her face with her hands. She has no strength left to continue the interview. Rose, a young nurse who has just entered on her rounds, takes her in her arms and caresses her. Susi is upset, and, not knowing what to do, says goodbye to Mireille. I take her into the living room and offer her a cup of tea.

'When you're ready...' I say, 'we can go to the first floor. They're expecting us.'

A woman on the oncology ward has asked to see the journalist. Her name is Angela and she's thirty-nine. She's bald and emaciated. She greets us with a smile and, turning round in her bed, looks Susi in the eye and says without preamble: 'Tomorrow I have a big operation, the third. I'm not sure I'll come out of it alive. When I heard last week about a visit from a journalist, I felt the need to talk. I was on tenterhooks because I was afraid you'd come after I'd already been under the knife.'

'I'm glad you want to talk to me. I want to ask you how you feel as you wait for your operation.'

'I'm really scared, but I also feel some hope: hope for a positive result that will allow me to believe in a cure. I'm not really afraid of dying, I'm more afraid of losing the prospect of the happiness I enjoyed for too short a time, and which the diagnosis of cancer cruelly cut short just when life seemed to be smiling. The oncologist told me that I'd been sick for several years, without the check-ups revealing the disease and letting them operate when the tumour was located only in the left breast. I had a thorough examination every year, but only last year did some of the results make my doctor ask for an in-depth evaluation on the oncology ward of the hospital, which, however, didn't confirm his suspicions. I think that, inside, I knew I was sick, but I didn't have the strength to cope with the disease, and so I hid it from myself and the doctors, letting go only when my partner came to live with me and I felt protected, loved and ready to face any ordeal. But I can't die now: I have to survive so that I can live with him, not just for a few months, but at least a few years. I'd hate to die now, because it would seem like betraying the expectations that have given my partner the strength to stay with me and love me completely, teaching him to make me happy, even in the face of death. Then again, to die is fine as long as I have the time to resolve issues still unsettled – remedying my difficult relation-ship with my father. I hope I still have a little time. And if I do die, I also fear for Edoardo. I'd like to give him some advice . . . Actually, no, that wouldn't be in good taste. I'll keep it for myself.'

Angela has nothing more to say to us for today. She smiles at us as the tears run down her face. Susi and I remain with her in silence. From the window we can see a field with sheep and some children who are running about, trying to climb onto their backs. One suc-ceeds then falls, and all the children shout, laughing. Their silvery voices are barely audible, but they seem to tell us that life goes on and they give us hope.

The round of interviews culminates in the dialysis unit. The patients here are regulars who meet three times a week in a large room with a dozen stations and complex machinery that in three or four hours purifies their blood, compensating for renal failure. Their general condition varies, and many of them suffer from other diseases. Some are diabetic, whereas others have heart problems. Some are hospitalized, others live in their own home or in a residence for the elderly. Both friendship and animosity exist in this room, and the various people assume different attitudes according to their respective predispositions to be cheerful, outgoing and optimistic, or sad, depressed and withdrawn.

Andy has asked to speak to us. He's an American citizen who has lived in Belgium for many years. He's a man in his seventies, a little overweight, who has loved life and still enjoys it as much as possible. He has a younger wife of about fifty-five whom he tries to provide with everything, as if he wants to be forgiven for being old and sick.

'I'm glad to see you,' he says to Susi. 'I want to tell you that, even though I have one foot in the grave, I'm not giving up, and I'm trying to make the best of what I have left of life. If you'd met me twenty years ago, you'd have seen another man. But my spirit is strong and my desire to live unshaken. I won't be coming to the hospital in the next two weeks, I'm taking my wife Diana to Waimea in Hawaii, and while I'm having my dialysis at the North Hawaii Community Hospital, she can enjoy a dream holiday at the Conrad Hotel. Next Saturday we're flying to San Diego, and from there a cruise ship will take us to Hawaii in four days. We're coming back by plane with a stopover in Atlanta. I'll also have dialysis twice on board the ship, and that will allow me to make a few exceptions to the strict diet set by my good Belgian doctors. However, between you and me, I don't take them too seriously, and that's all for the best. Why should I deprive myself of some treats? Just to live a bit longer? No, that's not my view, and I want to give Diana as pleasant a life as possible for the recognition I owe her. She loves me and supports me in spite of my condition, and she's certainly not doing it out of self-interest, waiting for me to kick the bucket. She's well off on her own account, and until two years ago had a successful job as vice-president of a multinational company operating in the field of alternative energy. Some time ago she filed a patent for a heat pump that she's profiting from like a gold mine. Good for her and for her two children — two great kids who are still under thirty, but who've already established themselves professionally. They're very attached to their mother and maybe Arthur will come to Waimea to introduce his girlfriend to Diana.'

Susi is surprised by this encounter, so different from the previous ones, and she stays to enjoy Andy's company for a few more minutes. The arrival of the doctor interrupts the conversation and I take Susi to a little living room to say goodbye and thank her for visiting. She says to me, 'This hospital is a world unto itself. From the outside I couldn't have imagined what I've discovered today. I think your work is as difficult as it is fascinating. It's been a day full of emotions and surprises. A day I won't forget. I hope I communicate to the readers and listeners what I've learned and the emotions I've experienced. Thank you!'

Susi goes away. Her visit has shaken me, making me recall an experience from twenty-five years ago. Inge, my partner, was dying at the Bordet Institute, a cancer hospital. Inge was a little over forty years old, but eight months of illness and treatments had made her lose weight and age prematurely. Her hair was beginning to grow back and this seemed to us like a promise of healing. A French journalist whose name I can't remember came to visit the hospital, saying that she was writing an essay called 'Men, and the Suffering of Women' and that she wanted to gather personal stories to include in her book. I don't know if the book was ever published. I recall with emotion that Inge wrote to her that she was aware of the imminence of death, but that nevertheless, the disease had allowed her to experience an intense and wonderful love, and to understand how important she was to the man she loved.

A Pilgrimage

Émile is a man of forty-five married to Céline, who is a little younger than him. We are old friends and have much in common. For many years we spent our holidays together in the mountains: Émile and Céline are sporty and have always kept fit. At times they would venture onto trails and alpine *vie ferrate* routes that I'd already given up attempting some time before, but afterwards we'd always meet up in a mountain hut, or at home in the evening, and chat for hours. For a couple of years Céline has been sick and is receiving treatment in a different hospital from the one where I work as a volunteer. The fact that Céline is in another hospital means I can be constant, diligent and caring in giving her support, spending many days with her and her loved ones, and sharing the hopes and suffering of a path I've already travelled. This wouldn't be possible in 'my' hospital, where volunteers can only be present on the ward during assigned hours, given that they are neither part of the patient's family nor can be considered their friends. We offer our time as a matter of solidarity, providing a listening service and assistance; we come and go as mere servants,[18] with no plans and no future. This is the great gift of the hospital volunteer service: it continually teaches us about compassion towards those who suffer, and a detachment from worldly things, while protecting us from an excessive attachment to the sick, or a personal involvement in their lives. But when the sick person is a friend or family member, the relationship is different from that of a simple servant.

Céline and Émile have been together for seventeen years and have two daughters, Béatrice and Barbara, aged fifteen and eleven respectively. The girls are sporty, sociable and cheerful like their parents. Now a teenager, Béatrice is already experiencing the excitement of the first adventures of adolescence. She is tall, with long, very attractive, black hair, which is her pride and joy. She tends to play mother to little Barbara, who is still – perhaps not for long – a plump little girl who plays with dolls and with the cat.

At present, Céline is hospitalized on an oncology ward after a fourth operation for pluri-metastatic breast cancer. Given her condition, a request has been made for her admission to the palliative care unit in the same hospital, where she may be transferred within days. Émile loves her deeply, which can be seen from the way he is always at hand, and from the intensity of his relationship. The oncology service nurses have taken a liking to him because he is so different from many of the other men who visit the hospital. He seems to be unafraid of illness and death, and dares to express his feelings towards Céline. When he arrives in her room, he often brings a flower or some other sign of his profound and sincere attachment, showing her how he continues to consider her the great love of his life, even though the disease has invaded and ravaged her body. He often passes Friday or Saturday night in her room, either in the armchair beside her, or in Céline's technological bed, where more than once the nurses have found them tenderly embraced. Now, after all the surgery and therapies that Céline has undergone in the last fourteen months, they are two well-known and respected individuals, whom all the health service personnel have become fond of.

Céline and Émile are two agnostic intellectuals. She's a neonatal paediatrician; he's a tax consultant specializing in international succession. Céline is aware of the gravity of her condition, but has not yet dared to talk about it explicitly with Béatrice and Barbara. About three weeks ago, it was Émile, together with the psychologist Lydie De Bast and Dr Joseph Deckers, an oncologist who has known Céline since their university days, who told her it was no longer useful to continue the chemotherapy, and that from then on, the doctors would only endeavour to relieve her pain and to help her without ever abandoning her. Céline cried in Émile's arms, and for a few days she was agitated and upset. The pain therapy relieves

Céline's suffering and is dosed so as to leave prolonged periods of consciousness, during which the effect of the opiates seems to give her a deep and intense sensitivity.

Émile has promised her that he'll continue to assist her and support her every wish, but he certainly didn't expect Céline to ask to go to Pietrelcina in Italy, the hometown of the famous Padre Pio. Out of a thousand possible requests, this is certainly the one that will prove most difficult for him to honour. Though himself an anticlerical agnostic, Émile has always been respectful of their friends who follow a spiritual path or attend a church. In fact, he almost envies those among their friends who've explored the mysterious allure of Eastern religions and had esoteric experiences in Tibet or India. But Pietrelcina for him represents a place of fanaticism and idolatry, the marketplace of salvation for those who let themselves be caught up in mass religious tourism in their eagerness for easy miracles. Émile is torn between the desire to respond to this extreme request by his wife, who is desperate at the prospect of her imminent death, and the need to maintain coherence in terms of their life choices, and not betray what had been one of their shared principles regarding non-religious certainties about the fundamental values in their lives. He feels he must refuse her, also in order to protect her from a lack of coherence that he believes has arisen not so much out of hope, and even less out of faith, but out of anguish and despair. To gain time, Émile tells her that, as a start, he will try to find out if and how it would be possible to organize the trip.

The social worker from the oncology unit is not surprised at Céline's request. Rash journeys of thousands of miles by dying patients are not uncommon. They travel far in search of their origins out of a deep need to belong to a history, or to rebuild old ties.[19] They also flee in the vain hope that Death will lose track of them.

Émile is therefore directed to Explorations and Discoveries, a travel agency run by young people who organize trips to spiritual holiday locations, including ones not on the traditional religious tourism circuit, and far removed from mass tourism based on sports activities, good food, or the pursuit of sexual encounters. The idea of Explorations and Discoveries appeals to Émile because the agency is not involved in organizing parish trips. This is a first step that won't force him into the bigoted world of those who seek miracles to reassure themselves and confirm their beliefs without faith, thrilled by what Émile considers to be primitive, magic rituals. His revulsion towards the Church is visceral in the most literal sense of the word. The intellectual violence he suffered as a child has injured him no less than the sexual violence we have heard so much about in recent times, but from which he was fortunately spared. In fact, his past actually prevents him from entering any church. Once, when he was already a grown man visiting a historic city in Spain, he went into a famous baroque cathedral. A service had just ended and had left the air saturated with incense, which brought back Émile's experience as a pre-teen altar boy. His stomach clenched and he had to rush outside to give vent to an explosion that seemed impatient to rid him of his recent breakfast and his old memories at one and the same time.

It's a Saturday morning and Émile has asked me to accompany him to the travel agency. Now that he's in this pleasant environment, he's attracted by distant destinations that evoke the idea of exploring the mystery of silence: a desert crossing between Morocco and Tunisia, a high-altitude trek in Tibet, or a stay in a Buddhist monastery in Myanmar. Yes, those would actually be acceptable destinations. But Pietrelcina! How would it be possible to go there without entering the world of sermons, simony, joyless hymns and the empty rituals that had poisoned his adolescent years?

'I think you're the prisoner of a painful experience that's left its mark,' says Sandra, the girl who has listened to Émile and, understanding his opposition, is showing us the agency's proposals. 'There's also a different way of reaching Pietrelcina from the one you imagine. A path where compassion and solidarity constitute the miracle in itself: not a cure, but the attainment of serenity. Next Saturday we're starting a trip for young people. Spend a few hours with us and perhaps you'll see an unexpected side to this pilgrimage that might encourage you to take a trip with your wife in search of inner peace.'

Explorations and Discoveries, with funding from a bank and the participation of a famous children's choir, is organizing a trip to Pietrelcina for thirty blind university students from the Oeuvre Nationale des Aveugles (National Association for the Blind). They'll be accompanied by the same number of young people from the choir, and by a dozen adults, including doctors, nurses and entertainers, as well as two choirmasters. Most of the blind students are in good health, except for six who are suffering from various serious conditions that will affect their survival in the medium term, but for now do not prohibit a degree of autonomy and freedom of movement. For many of the blind young people, this will be the first long absence from home without their family members, whereas the boys in the choir are accustomed to concert tours, some of which even take them beyond national borders. Yet this trip is also a new experience for them too. Each one has been assigned the challenging task of accompanying and assisting one of the young blind students, of being at his disposal, and, above all, of helping him to become a 'singing' member of their community of singers.

During the month before the trip, three meetings have been contemplated to prepare everything, and create an initial contact between the two groups of boys.

Émile has been invited to the first meeting, which will take place next Saturday at 11:00 a.m. in the association's hall. The second meeting is scheduled for the following Sunday, and the third, fifteen days later.

At the first meeting, Aline, a teacher at the high school for the blind who will accompany the young people on the journey, briefly presents both a history of Padre Pio and the trip arrangements. Padre Pio was a twentieth-century friar born Francesco Forgione, who even during his lifetime was the subject of mass veneration of impressive proportions. A controversial and much discussed figure, some consider him to have been a miracle worker whilst others consider him a mere impostor. News of inexplicable events created an aura of the miraculous around him, which attracted crowds, large donations, and many speculations fuelled by widespread credulity. It also aroused serious doubts and reservations among the Vatican hierarchy. Aline explains that the trip, which will require two coaches, is to last eight days: four for the journey there and back, with five nights in Pietrelcina at one of the numerous hotels around the Capuchin monastery where Padre Pio lived, which have sprung up as a result of the speculation the pilgrimages have inspired.

Émile plans to return the following Sunday morning to find out how the trip will be organized, but most of all to understand how the 'compassion and solidarity' that Sandra mentioned will become part of the programme.

On that same Saturday, Béatrice and Barbara go to visit their mother in hospital. They're independent and self-possessed enough to use public transport on their own. Visiting hours on the oncology ward are very broad: between 11:00 a.m. and 9:00 p.m. In addition, in the case of patients like Céline in single rooms, it's also possible to stay overnight. They're happy to visit their mother for once without the perhaps overly protective presence of their father. Émile has asked me to go to the hospital in the morning, knowing that he'll be busy at the travel agency. I see the girls arrive around noon. I greet them affectionately and take my leave of Céline, who is looking forward to this visit with great emotion. She plans to tell the girls that she is reaching the end, and she has talked with me about how to do this. She is too weak for such a difficult encounter and is afraid of not finding the right words. But then, are there any right words for telling two young daughters that their mother is dying?

'How lovely you are!' she says spontaneously when she sees them come in.

At this point I decide it's better to leave the girls alone with their mother. I know it will be an emotional visit during which they will exchange spontaneous words of love, hope and anguish that an external ear should not hear – even that of a discreet friend.

In the late afternoon, Émile comes to collect his daughters from the hospital. He remains for a short while with them beside Céline, who seems to be asleep and is wearing a serene, relaxed expression. Her face radiates sweetness and tranquillity. Having found the strength to declare her approaching end, an ineffable well-being has settled deep, very deep within her heart, that she'd call happiness if the word didn't seem to her inadequate in the circumstances. But what is happiness? At her core, Céline knows. She was twenty-two years old when she held Émile in her arms and knew that this man was the rock on which she would build her life, and that their love was the meaning she would give to her life. And again, at Béatrice's first cry, holding her to her breast, Céline understood that her own happiness would lie in giving her unconditional love to this child she had borne, as she accompanied her on her road to independence and freedom. Yes, Céline knows that for her, happiness is to be cognizant of the meaning of her life and to live to achieve it. Céline is able to acknowledge that she is happy in the face of death.

The father and daughters arrive home. Together the girls set about preparing a good dinner, inventing a variation on the theme of prawns in sweet and sour sauce, which they had eaten at a Thai restaurant. Émile decides not to go to the hospital this evening. It seems to him that at this moment his place is with his daughters.

'What's this story about Padre Pio that mum was talking about?' Barbara asks at dinner.

Émile explains that he has promised to grant Céline's every wish. The girls mention to him that their mother told them she no longer thinks she needs this, and that she plans to speak to him about it tomorrow.

The sweet and sour prawns are a great success and remind them of a dinner the four of them shared a couple of months before. It creates an atmosphere of intimacy in which the girls talk at length about their visit to their mother.

In the weeks after her death, to help the girls deal with their bereavement and express their emotions and grief, Émile often spoke with them about what they had experienced and shared that day. Of the two daughters, Barbara was the most eager to talk, whereas Béatrice, although participating emotionally in the memories, kept to herself the secret of her last meeting with her mother. It was providential that Émile had given them the opportunity to be alone with her for a few hours, allowing the three of them to talk freely. The repeated reconstruction of those dramatic hours gave Émile the sensation of having been present himself at their meeting, and also of being able to recount every moment and share it with me. I felt it was good for him to talk about it again. From what he told me, I'm able to reconstruct that emotional afternoon.

Once she was alone with her daughters, Céline broke the ice by saying that she would have liked to take a walk in the park with them and have a coffee in the sun at Chalet Robinson.

'By the way, have you been there since it reopened after the fire?'

'Yes,' Barbara replied, 'Bertrand invited us to the Chalet with his children. It's a nice place, but they seemed very embarrassed in our company, as if they wanted to say something without finding the courage to do it.'

Perhaps thinking that Barbara was hinting, Céline felt that it was a good opportunity to open up and tell them what she knew of her condition.

'I can understand that Bertrand was embarrassed. He wanted to prepare you for the idea that I won't be able to get well and that you'll be without a mother soon. It's hard for me, too, to talk to you about it, but I feel that today is the right time to face what seems to be in store for us.'

The girls sit on the bed, one on each side of their mother, who feels them close and caresses them. She tells them she feels reasonably well, but has no illusions about being able to get better. Céline describes her present state as a break in her journey, a momentary relief, which allows her to feel well enough to be with her 'little girls' for just enough time for all of them to say everything that fills their hearts.

'Until yesterday I thought I'd be able to get well. Now I have the serene awareness of being close to the end.'

Céline knows she has no time to waste and that she still has something to do. Until then, she'd believed in the possibility of regaining her health, even if it were by means of a miracle. Fortunately, it will no longer be necessary to ask Émile to take her to Padre Pio's convent in Italy. She's realized on her own that there's no need to seek the impossible, and that it is better to find serenity in the simple acceptance of her fate. She's had everything she could have wanted from life and is now at peace because she's realized her dream of love.

Céline says she's ready to go, saddened only by not being able to see her daughters grow up or offer them support in their lives as young women. She tells them to trust Émile, who loves all three of them very much, and to have confidence in him — in his advice and in his decisions, also should he find a new partner when she's gone. 'Émile has loved me deeply, and together we learned that the way to share hopes and dreams is by listening to one's life companion and seeking happiness together. It's a lesson that won't make him a prisoner, venerating my memory, but will remain in his heart, helping him in the life he has before him.'

Béatrice and Barbara listen without speaking. Tears run down their cheeks, wetting Céline's pillow. They feel a sense of emptiness, as if they were on the edge of an abyss. They have a clear awareness of living a crucial moment in their lives. Béatrice moves even closer to her mother and kisses her cheeks, wetting her with her tears. She tells her she loves her and asks her not to leave her alone. If she goes, who will she tell her secrets to?

The girls see Céline slip into a state of semi-consciousness, which is the first phase of coma. The intensity of the meeting, heart-breaking yet sweet, is more than Céline can bear. But she is not totally absent, and hears her beloved daughters' words as if they come from far away.

Barbara caresses Céline's face and her small fingers stop on her lips. Barbara feels a vibration, a sign of life and of love, as if her mother were trying to kiss her. She begins to cry, sobbing, holding on to her mother as if she wanted to keep her and protect her. Béatrice strokes her sister's head, trying to relieve her suffering and make her feel that they are together in facing the death of their mother. Touching their mother's still face with their lips, they murmur tender words of love, recalling moments when they felt closest and most connected to her. At times the words are dis-connected and only make sense to those who know the secret code of their intimate communication.

Barbara has told Émile that Béatrice, through her tears, whispered to her mother that she was hopelessly in love with Mario, Bertrand's eldest son. She told her that he is shy and has never declared to her what he has otherwise tried to let her know in a thousand ways through his constancy and attentions. It is so new and so great an experience for Béatrice that she'd wanted to have the joy and comfort of sharing it with her mother. Barbara then says with provocative spontaneity that she'd confessed to her mother that she was afraid that if she dies, Émile will bring home another wife and that she will be as unkind as Aline is to Vincent's sons. If this happens, Barbara told her mother, and then repeated to Émile, she will run away where no one can find her.

Céline heard these conversations, but her body had become heavy like sand. She could no longer utter a single word or move a hand or her legs, nor even blink, as if all the weight of the world was on her. At first she heard the beloved voices from a great distance, then she let herself sink into the dark depths of coma.

Scared at seeing their mother in this state, the girls ran to call Michelle, an efficient, attentive and patient nurse who had long since been able to gain their complete confidence. Michelle hurried to Céline's bedside. She explained to the girls that it could be a temporary effect of the pain therapy, and probably their mother was not as absent as her appearance might suggest. She advised them to take her hand and talk to her. She was not sure that their mother could hear everything, but in any case, talking to her would do them good.

'Each of you spend a quarter of an hour with your mum, one at a time. You'll see that it will be a really special, meaningful time together.'

It was a shared time that later remained in their hearts together with all the harrowing events of those terrible days; one that they wanted to share with their father that same evening, and which they continued to recall in the weeks following their mother's death.

The following day, Émile decides not to attend the second meeting regarding the trip and to go instead to the hospital. He wants to tell Céline that he has found an agency that could organize a trip to Pietrelcina, far removed from any religious hysteria.

Céline has passed a quiet night. She wakes around nine, and when Émile enters the room is still half-sleep. With an effort of will, she forces herself awake in order to be present at a meeting that might be one of the last. Émile goes to her and kisses her gently.

He says, 'Last night you were asleep when I came to pick up the girls. At home they cooked me Thai prawns in sweet and sour sauce, like those we once ate together in Rhode-Saint-Genèse. They're starting to feel at home in the kitchen and it's a pleasure to see them work and create together.'

'I remember almost nothing about yesterday,' Céline replies, 'but it seems to me that they were with me for a long time. Sometimes I fall into a state of profound unconsciousness. I'm glad to be awake today because I have to tell you something. It's wonderful to still feel the need to tell something, or have things to say to each other after all these years!'

Céline cries as she tells him she knows that a cure is impossible for her. She has stopped deluding herself, but feels serene and ready. She's given up the idea of the journey of hope to Padre Pio; indeed, she's almost ashamed to have wanted it, and apologizes for having asked him for it. She no longer needs to get better because her earthly journey is done. She's understood that she is not the patient with breast cancer in room 1542. Nor is she the metastases to the lungs and liver. These inhabit her and have taken up an increasingly large space in her body. But Céline is more than her illness. She is the mother of Barbara and Béatrice and Émile's wife. All this and more besides, as if all the ailments that the disease has inflicted on her had finally freed her from her conditioning. Now all that is left of Céline is something bigger than herself. She is leaving sickness and suffering behind her, and is taking with her the more intense and richer part of her life: the memories of the tears and smiles of all the children she has treated, and all the experiences of love, sharing and forgiveness that have given meaning to her life. Soon she'll know the mystery of life and human destiny. She recalls the story of Momo, which she read to her daughters at bedtime. Émile, together with Béatrice and Barbara, will be with her to share her experience. They'll become immortal because she keeps them inside her, in the love that unites them.[20]

Céline is ready.

'Please recline the back of the bed. Take my hands in yours. I'm going to let myself go.'

Céline's funeral was an intense secular ceremony, held in the meadows of the Woluwe-Saint-Pierre cemetery in Wezembeek-Oppem — a celebration of solidarity that included many people dear to her, many parents of infants she had treated, and her own doctors, who only very rarely accompany their patients to their final resting place. Songs of love and fellowship moved all those present, and emotional speeches evoked and honoured the most significant moments of Céline's life.

Émile has passed on to the two girls the legacy of love and serenity that Céline left him. Now that they've lost Céline, they are united and allow themselves to cry, but they don't indulge in the sadness of mourning. Life goes on.

Dignity

Marina is a forty-five-year-old cancer patient with a serious, long-term psychotic disorder. She arrived on the ward heavily sedated, but, as a result of analgesic therapy, after two days she begins to have periods of wakefulness and awareness during which we start to get to know her. Once fully conscious, she told the doctor she would refuse any cancer therapy or any medical treatment whatsoever.

Now, she no longer complains of the pains, which once tormented her. Basically, she asks to be left alone in peace. She says to the auxiliary nurses who come to wash her and make her bed, 'Leave me in peace! Don't touch me.'

Assisting patients means walking by their side, leaving them free to choose the direction and speed of their steps.[21] Sometimes it's not easy, and this is where our vision of the dignity of a human being is tested. The challenge is to acknowledge and demonstrate through our behaviour the inalienable dignity of the person who is before us, even when that person is extremely infirm.

When Marina was in a coma during the past days, there was no problem in caring for her and washing her; the bed was regularly remade and her personal hygiene assured. But today Marina is awake and she defends herself vigorously from any kind of assistance. Her features are small, regular and extremely gaunt. Her gaze is enigmatic at times and seems to conceal a mystery. Her general condition has deteriorated and she is incontinent. There is a strong smell of excrement in her room, but this doesn't seem to bother her.

Ines, the young auxiliary nurse, has asked an experienced colleague to give her a hand. Together, they enter the room and Ines gently offers to remake the bed and change the sheets. Marina obsessively repeats, 'Don't touch me! Leave me in peace! Don't touch me!'

The nurses withdraw, telling Marina to call them if she needs them. I wonder about the significance of 'Don't touch me!', and in this case what it means to respect her will and adapt our behaviour to it. We discuss Marina in the team meeting. I believe she is not in full possession of her mental faculties and that action is justified — indeed, recommendable. Not everyone agrees. I say that when babies struggle and cry when we change them, we wouldn't dream of not cleaning them, even when they make it clear they don't like it. We decide to try again with the utmost delicacy.

I go into Marina's room and sit down beside her bed. The headboard and pillows support her in an almost seated position. She is holding her head upright and her eyes are open and alert. I tell her my name and that I am a volunteer, and ask if I can stay with her for a moment. She is very thin, her face pale and emaciated. She looks me straight in the eye quite aggressively. I hold her gaze for a long while without speaking. I try to look at her with gentleness, and to express through my gaze my desire to remain close to her and help her. After what seems a very long time, she says to me quite sternly, 'Don't touch me.'

I don't let this bother me; instead I smile and say to her, 'Okay.'

We remain facing each other for a while.

I continue to wonder what Marina means by 'Don't touch me', and what memories and suffering are evoked. Her repeated forced hospitalization in the closed wards of the psychiatric services must have left wounds that have not healed. Will we be able to convince her that she can trust the hospital staff? There's a game I play with my grandchildren, a kind of challenge. We see who can stare longest at the other without laughing. This situation is very different. It requires trying to see beyond a barrier that suffering and illness have created around the woman who is here with me — a barrier that suggests the humiliations that Marina has suffered; the endless struggle with the treacherous and mysterious affliction that has compromised her mental faculties, together with the fear of new treatments and new suffering. I continue to hold her gaze. I sense her fear, but I no longer see the aggression that was there initially. I think I've made a small step forward. Marina seems tired, and after a while she looks away from me and watches the trees outside the window.

I remain in the room for a long time without speaking. Marina no longer stares at me intently and seems lost in her own thoughts.

She asks me, 'Where's Pierrot?'

I don't know who Pierrot is. I say to her, 'I don't know. To tell you the truth, I don't know him.'

Marina says nothing, but she gives the impression she doesn't believe me. After a while she leans towards me as if to tell me a secret and says, 'He must have fallen asleep as usual. You can't rely on him.'

Then I see that Marina's eyes are starting to close. She seems tired. She makes an effort to keep her eyes open. Later, she falls asleep. I leave the room.

It's the end of my shift and I go home. I'm back on the same ward two days later. In the meantime Marina has died. At the meeting they tell me that the day before she went into a coma. Nurses were able to make the bed and care for her. She never regained consciousness again.

I feel frustrated when I experience dramatic situations, and then, when I go back on the ward, find that a relationship I've tried to build has been interrupted and ended forever. It teaches me a lesson in humility and makes me content to live in the present with the patients, without wanting to make plans regarding them, and without being certain of tomorrow.

Ave Maria

It was Tunç, an old man of Turkish origin who had been living in Brussels for a long time, who was my tutor when I first arrived on the palliative care ward some years ago. There are thirty volunteers: when a new one arrives, he or she is taken under the wing of a senior volunteer, who acts as a tutor for a certain period of time in order to explain the principles of the role and introduce the new person to the hospital staff, and to the customs and etiquette of the ward. Tunç and I have remained close through genuine friendship, and we also see one another outside of ward meetings and training days. With him I shared a personal experience that takes me back to when I was one of the patients in hospital.

The patient in the first bed in room 560 is called Barbara. She's dying from lung cancer that has now become generalized. She's sixty-five years old and has never smoked. Her cancer is one of those sad cases of disease caused by passive smoking. For about twenty years when she was still young, she worked in a post office where several colleagues smoked one cigarette after another, polluting the workplace. For years Barbara had bronchitis and a cough, and four years ago she was diagnosed with cancer of the right lung. Today, a law bans smoking in public offices, but for Barbara it's too late. Her days are numbered, yet she is drawing close to death with surprising serenity.

As Tunç has noted on other occasions, she has her eyes closed, but that doesn't mean she's asleep. Tunç enters the room quietly and speaks softly to Assunta, the woman occupying the other bed, telling her that today, I'm here too, a novice volunteer.

Assunta is happy to hear that I'm a fellow countryman, and she says to me in Italian, 'When I was young I was a cook at the Italian Embassy in Belgium.'

'That's wonderful,' I say. 'I hope you'll feel like giving me some of your secret recipes.'

Assunta replies, 'When there was an important lunch with twenty or thirty guests and a dish was particularly successful, the ambassador's wife used to make me come into the dining room and the guests would applaud me. But if some lady should ask for the recipe, my instructions were to give it reluctantly and imprecisely to avoid it being copied. But I stopped working many years ago, and now at home I only cook simple dishes.'

'So much the better,' I say, 'that way they'll be within my range. Let me have the recipe for one of your secret dishes that's easy to prepare.'

She thinks about it then tells me, 'Rigatoni with sauce. Prepare the sauce as usual with onion, garlic, celery and carrots, white wine – and tomato of course – and at the end dissolve one ounce of gorgonzola dolce cheese per person. A guaranteed success.' She stops for a moment, then asks Tunç in French: 'But what does a volunteer actually do?'

'I've been a volunteer for many years and I don't know how to do anything,' says Tunç in reply, taking advantage of the situation to give me a lesson on the type of job I'm learning. 'And I don't have to do anything; in fact, I'm required to do nothing. But doing nothing doesn't prevent me from being here and keeping you company. Volunteers don't have to invent activities to liven up the patients' day. They wait in silence beside the sick in the expectation and hope that their suffering will become a word, a dialogue or an encounter. If this happens, the volunteers listen to the patients' requests and accompany them on their journey.'

Without opening her eyes, Barbara tells Tunç: 'You have a particular accent, like a friend of mine's husband who's Turkish by origin, but has been living in Brussels for thirty years. He's called Tunk; maybe you know each other?'

'It might be me,' says Tunç. 'My wife's name is Mireille. My name is Tunç, which you pronounce with a soft "ç", like in "cherry".'

Barbara opens her eyes and smiles.

'I thought I recognized you yesterday, but I wasn't sure and didn't know how to make certain. Once, you came to my house to pick up Mireille after she'd spent some time with me. I remember you talked about Kayseri, your hometown, and you said that President Abdullah Gül was born there too. It's been almost two years since that day. Back then I wasn't really that unwell, even though I'd just come home from hospital. Just imagine, I thought everything was all right and that the surgery had healed me. I counted my chickens too soon. Now they've informed me there's nothing more to be done. It was Dr Malder who told me and explained it all to me, promising that he'll assist me to the end. He's really a wonderful man. He was able to reassure me even while he was telling me there's no hope of a recovery. He knows how to communicate the truth to patients who want to understand their condition, allowing us to wait for death mindfully, without giving up on life ahead of time. Ask Mireille if she wants to come to see me one of these days, I've got something important to tell her. And if she does agree to come, tell her not to wait too long.'

Tunç sits down next to Barbara and promises to speak to Mireille. Barbara is afraid she's offended him with her comment about his accent, but Tunç reassures her and tells her they're even because he corrected her pronunciation of his name. Tunç explains that even though he's made many efforts to learn to speak French properly during the thirty years he's lived in Belgium, he actually doesn't mind showing an obvious sign of his origin, which he's particularly proud of. He tells her that in Europe there are many prejudices and wrong opinions about Turkey and the Turks, and that his country is not sufficiently well known by many of its detractors. Barbara has been to Turkey several times and enjoys hearing him talk about it. She particularly remembers Ephesus, and the house of Mary the mother of Jesus on Nightingale Mountain. She went there the first time in 1979, when she was thirty. She tells Tunç it was a memorable trip, which also happened to coincide with a visit by Pope

Wojtyla. Tunç tells her that there have been Christians in his family for two generations and that he also paid an emotional visit to Mary's house, which he advises visiting out of season when the crowds of tourists from Bodrum's beaches are not around to disturb the tranquillity of the sacred place.

Assunta now joins the conversation and tells us that she once visited Istanbul on a lightning, three-day trip with tickets the ambassador had given as a prize. Assunta thinks it's the most fascinating city of all those she's visited, so much so that she's asked her husband to take her back there when she's better. Tunç is pleased to know that the two women love his country. He promises that tomorrow he'll bring *pişmaniye*, cakes made of sugar, flour and butter. He's taught Mireille how to make them and assures us they're just like the ones his mother used to make.

The next day it's Mireille herself who brings them when she comes to the hospital, responding quickly to Barbara's invitation. Mireille is perhaps ten years older than Barbara, but she's in good health and even seems younger than her. It's been quite a while since they've seen one another, but their old rapport returns at once, as if they'd been together only yesterday. Towards the end of the 1980s, they spent eighteen months in Lomé, Togo, on a United Nations project. At the time, Mireille was an FAO agent, whereas Barbara was sent as a logistics co-operator by the Belgian administration. They worked on a water resources and drinking water project. Barbara had learned the rudiments of the Ewe language and knew how to establish a relationship with the villagers, managing to communicate with them and gain their trust. It was a difficult and intense time during which the two women became intimate friends. Afterwards, they'd lost touch, and only Barbara's illness has reunited them.

Mireille had not thought that Barbara would be so close to the end and so rushes to the hospital as soon as possible after receiving the invitation via Tunç. She chooses to go there at about 7 p.m., an hour she knows will be very quiet, and conducive to a meeting that she has contemplated with a certain emotional anxiety. Barbara welcomes her with her usual simplicity, as if she'd invited her to her home for a cup of tea.

'I didn't know Tunç worked here,' she says. I was glad to see him and, through him, to have the chance to see you. You were right to come quickly; I feel I've only got a few days left. I recently made an important discovery and I was looking for someone to share it with before I go.'

Barbara stops, as if searching for the words to express her emotion. Mireille strokes one of her hands and waits until Barbara starts to speak again, this time without stopping.

'When I heard Tunç's voice, I thought of you and our private conversations in Africa. I said to myself that you'd know how to listen to me. When I'm alone, I think of the people I've met and the experiences that have made me grow, preparing me now to live the end of my life serenely. When we were in Togo, I was fascinated by the animist religion, even if in my own way I continued to belong to the Catholic Church. In fact, I adopted some aspects of animism. I'm convinced that for me animism is a way of objectifying certain perceptions we have inside, a way of giving them substance as it were — if that weren't a contradiction in terms. In this way, we put ourselves in touch with reality, or with people who are distant or dead, but who still live in our hearts. In this sense I believe in some form of existence after death. We'll go on living in the hearts and minds of those who loved us. I don't know if after death I'll be aware of being present in the world through my loved ones' memories, but I know that, for now, it's important for me to be aware that around me are people I've loved and who've loved me. It's like a birthday party I've invited my loved ones to, then surprise guests turn up unexpectedly. I don't mean to say that this room is full of ghosts, but that my heart welcomes and recalls all the experiences of love in my life, and all the relationships that have given it meaning. But I must tell you about my discovery. I already told you that many years ago I was ecstatically moved during a visit to Mary's house in Ephesus.

Since then, I've continued the habit of reciting a Hail Mary every night before I fall asleep. I know inside me that the mother of Jesus is with me throughout this vigil, because for many years I asked her to 'pray for me at the hour of my death'. I feel inhabited by her presence; she's the one who'll ferry me to the other side, who'll help me to reach the other shore when the time comes. What will happen afterwards, no one knows, but I think I'll be at peace. I believe it's necessary to die, also to make room for others[22] and give them the opportunity to see how welcoming and beautiful the world is — the mark and sign of a God who is the supreme good — and how deep the relationships are that people are able to weave between one another, creating bonds that even transcend the barrier of death.'

Barbara falls silent while Mireille continues to hold her right hand in hers. It has grown dark, and from the window only the lights of the neighbourhood can be seen in the distance, along with the occasional flash of headlights as a car crosses the speed bump at the entrance to the hospital. Tears run down Barbara's cheeks, pausing between the wrinkles that mark her face, then continuing down again along her neck like a river of emotions overflowing its bed. Mireille and Assunta also cry silently and appear to be listening to the song of the vision that is accompanying Barbara on her last journey.

Returning home late that night, Mireille tells Tunç about her visit to Barbara and her serenity as she waits for death. Tunç is moved by this, and at the first opportunity tells me about it with great circumspection, perhaps afraid that I won't know how to capture Barbara's mood and may interpret her story as an hallucination, or a form of religiosity bordering on the cult of magic.

I am, however, prepared to accept this testimony of spiritual presences, which takes me back to something I experienced at least twenty years ago. At the time, I had distanced myself considerably from the Catholic Church and had found a spiritual path that suited me in India, where for ten years I spent my holidays in an ashram, continuing the practice of meditation and chanting when I was back in Brussels. I was attracted by a different kind of spirituality, based on detecting the presence of God within me and in the people around me, and I refused the beliefs proposed dogmatically by the Roman Church, which, in my view, appropriates for itself unjustified exclusivity in indicating the path to salvation.

I was rushed to the Erasme Hospital, one of the largest university hospitals in Brussels, because of severe haemorrhaging. I manifested abdominal pain that led to fears of colon cancer. I felt exhausted and thought I was close to death. Ultimately, I was content and ready to accept death and follow into the next world my partner who had left me prematurely a short time before. Three or four long days passed before the mysterious and reassuring diagnosis of ameboma was made — a rare, non-degenerative, infectious tumorous disease, treatable with medication. In the days of uncertainty prior to the diagnosis, I was confined to bed, attached to drips and catheters, and feeling very weak. It was hot. I wore lightweight, green Punjabi pyjamas, purchased in Ganeshpuri, which are cooler than cotton ones. I discovered that they had the power to create a special relationship with the nurses, who confused them — perhaps because of the colour — with surgeons' coats. One after the other I played cassettes of mantra music on my little stereo as I prepared for death by reading the Book of Job. At a certain point, when one cassette had just finished, in the silence could be heard the growing sound of a group of musicians from far away playing *Ohm na mu bagavate Muktanandaya*, one of the mantras that enliven the ashram in Ganeshpuri. I felt that Baba Muktananda was coming to fetch me in person and take me with him to enlightenment. I jumped out of bed and ran towards the hallway singing. The two drip stands I was attached to fell to the ground, hampering my movement. In the hallway there was only one nurse, who looked at me in surprise. There was no sign of Muktananda, nor could the mantra be heard any longer. The nurse brought me back into the room, scolding me for getting up. Then, seeing my stereo on the bedside table, she asked, 'What are these chants that you listen to all the time?'

'They're mantras, prayers of Indian spirituality.'

'But you can't!' said the nurse with an innocent spontaneity that was even more surprising given that we were in a hospital attached to the secular ULB (Université libre de Bruxelles). This reaction spoke volumes about the power of the Catholic Church's conditioning and the fear of diversity.

A few minutes later I had a visitor. It was a member of the spiritual group of the disciples of Muktananda. I realized that the music that had made me leap out of bed had come from her car radio as she passed under the windows of the building on the way to the car park. I felt upset and disappointed. I needed to reflect and closed my eyes. Slowly, I realized that there was no reason to be disappointed. The peace I thought Muktananda would lead me to was already inside me. I could open my eyes and welcome my visitor. I felt like crying. I said something unintelligible about the gift she'd given me. My message was not clear, but it showed that I was at peace and not afraid of a diagnosis that could be devastating.

She stayed to keep me company in silence, then left without having said a word. She didn't understand much of what had happened, but realized that, without knowing it, she'd given me a gift.

The Wait

Marco, an artist and friend of my father's, is ninety-four years old. He's an old mountain-dweller whose only ailment is old age, *ipsa morbus,* an infirmity in itself. Every time I'm in Italy and visit him, he looks at me with his lively blue eyes and asks me, smiling, 'Did you bring the injection?'

Jokingly, he tells me that his wait for death has gone on too long and that he would like my help to get it over with, given that in Belgium, where I live, euthanasia has been decriminalized. He pretends to believe that in Belgium, barbiturates and neuro-muscular paralysing agents such as Thiopental and Norcuron® are on sale at the supermarket.

His request is really his need to be reassured and to hear it said that he still has a role to play in his family, and that his daughter and grandchildren love him.

One of his grandsons, Denis, now thirty, is a ski instructor and trainer for the women's national ski team. I tell Marco that I remember well when Denis was four years old and Marco took him by the hand up on a path behind the house. Marco gets excited and says, 'I'm the one who taught him to ski! In my day there were no lifts or snowmobiles. In those days the mountain was only for those who conquered it, climbing it on sealskins. I know all the mountains in our valleys, rock by rock. I've been to Rome and Paris, but I only feel at home in my own town. But now I can't even get down the stairs! It is time to switch off the motor. Have you brought me the injection?'

'I've brought a box of *Côte d'Or* chocolates. They're a Belgian speciality that you can buy without a prescription and offer to people who come to visit you. The injection's not for you; there are still too many people who love you and come to visit you to see your paintings and hear your stories of the war, or the mountain legends.'

In fact, Marco has no desire to die; he just wants to provoke me with his request because he expects me to say that his life still has meaning and that it's a pleasure to come and see him.

Marco tells me about my parents. In his memory he idealizes and honours them.

'Your father came to visit me and sat in the sun on the bench outside the front door of the house. I sat down next to him and we looked at the mountains to the north, coloured pink by the last rays of the sun, or to the west, towards the Latemar, where the sun goes to hide. Your father Mario asked me the names of all the peaks, and now and then he'd ask me to test him on them, to see if he could remember. He was called up during the Great War, beginning as a recruit in Piedmont at the age of eighteen and continuing in Rome as a second lieutenant. I was enlisted at the same age, in 1940, during World War II, and I managed to stay in the barracks at Bolzano for three years. I was a corporal in the Alpinists.'

It's a story I've heard before and one that Marco likes to tell. He was commissioned to paint phrases dear to il Duce, such as 'Believe, Obey, Fight' or 'We Will Win', above the main door of the barracks and on the walls of the houses at the entrances to towns. Some of the ones along the SS12 state highway remained visible for a long time afterwards.

'The truth is, under Mussolini things were much better than they are now.'

He likes to tease me and start a lively discussion on politics and Italy's future. Because I live in Brussels, he thinks I know all about what government propaganda is concealing from the unsuspecting Italian citizens. I give him enough rope and jokingly tell him that Italy is colonized by three superpowers that have backed the Italian governments of the last sixty years: the United States, the Vatican and organized crime. I explain that an indirect and certainly incomplete proof of this can be seen in the symbol that, for a couple of years now, has been introducing the news on the Italian TV channel, RAI 1 in the form of Ratzinger and Obama's icons – which appear before President Napolitano's. This theory appeals to Marco and he says he'll mention it to the parish priest who often comes to visit him. He tells me it will be a way of livening up a visit which otherwise risks focusing mainly on religious topics that he is neither competent nor interested in discussing.

'You see, Marco, you're not ready for the injection. You'll have to keep going for a long time yet.'

'I know,' he replies, 'but I think it's going on a bit too long. Your mother joined your father only a few weeks after his death. I was left alone two years ago. I wasn't even fit to go to Agnese's funeral. I'm always stuck here at home. Now I can't even manage to go down to my studio to paint. All that's left for me is the catalogue of my works, which are more than four thousand. Everything is written in this book, including the buyer's name. A few weeks ago a man came from Vercelli with one of my paintings of Lake Carezza. He wanted a certificate of authenticity. I found the picture in this register; it was a canvas from 1968.'

'What year did you exhibit in Paris?' I ask.

'I think it was 1975. What a thrill! It was a good time but I was glad to get home. I'm not a globetrotter like you.'

'In your heart you have a world of images and memories that are always at hand to keep you company. What's your fondest memory?'

Marco takes his time before answering. He drinks a drop of water, coughs, sputters, then, beating the ground repeatedly with the end of his stick, he tells me:

'I'd gone to Rome for a show and didn't know where to sleep. An old client from my inn had left me his address and I went to his house. He welcomed me like a brother and made me sleep in his bed while he slept on a sofa in the dining room. There was no way he'd allow me to refuse his offer and let me sleep on the sofa instead. I gave him a picture of Lagusel to return the favour. I never saw him again, but I'll never forget his welcome. You can't imagine what it's like for someone from the mountains to find himself in a big city where there are more houses than trees, and the only animals you see are cats.'

It's grown late. Marco's favourite daughter, Denis's mother, has come to take him to bed. Marco and I hug. As he says goodbye to me, he becomes emotional and thanks me for visiting him. In order not to let me see he's crying, he says gruffly, 'Next time, don't forget the injection.'

Another person who says that the wait for the end has gone on too long is Norine, a woman of ninety, condemned by a generalized cancer, but stabilized in a pain-free condition during a stay on our ward. She has since been moved to a nursing home near Brussels, where they are continuing to treat her according to the pain relief programme established by our doctors. Norine is not able to walk, but with a little help she can manage to move to an armchair for an hour or two each day. She is as small and light as a little girl, and so she's easy to move without any effort. Her hair is white and rather thin, her face delicate and wrinkle-free. She has no teeth left, but this doesn't stop her from smiling. She has a son, already retired, who has moved to the south Ardennes and comes to visit her from time to time. When he heard that his mother's stay in the hospital would soon be over, he diligently searched left and right until he found a nursing home about twenty kilometres from the capital. Norine has asked him to sell her house in Uccle, where she's been living alone since she was widowed many years ago. She's also told him to take or sell everything that's in the house, asking him only to keep some of her books, which she can no longer read, but which are still dear to her and she'd like to see remain in good hands. Norine has had a suitcase brought to the nursing home containing her nightgowns, a dressing gown, some shawls, a vanity case and a number of photographs in elegant wooden frames. It's all she thinks she might need. She's requested that her son take the suitcase away, saying, 'There'll be no luggage on the next trip.'

She left the hospital in an ambulance, a little sad at leaving our ward where she'd established a good relationship with a number of the nurses, and especially with Françoise, the physiotherapist whose massages gave her a feeling of well-being, despite being so fatigued by age and infirmity. Norine has great sensitivity and an intense spiritual life. Nearing death, she now feels free to express what she would never have dared to say about her choice of an alternative spirituality to that of the dominant culture. She is in contact with spiritual entities whose beneficial presence she feels, and she tells of experiences and visions that have accompanied her all her life. She has led a very fulfilling life, and has now freed herself of all her possessions, separating from worldly things like a wise person who has reached nirvana. She is ready to pass away, waiting for the moment serenely but with some impatience.

Although she's distanced herself from practising the Catholic religion, she has retained a personal relationship with Christ and Mary. One of her neighbours in the nursing home brought Norine a small cross and hung it near her bed. She also suggested and has since organized a visit from a priest, who will administer the sacrament of the anointing of the sick. Norine does not know whether to talk to him about her spiritual reading and study of the apocryphal gospels, which she greatly enjoyed when she was still able to read. Now that she no longer can, she remains alone, motionless in her bed, finding peace and serenity in her personal and heterodox spirituality. Her neighbour has great faith, she tells me. She has strongly recommended the priest whose visit is now imminent, describing to Norine the benefits of receiving the sacrament of the sick that she herself has experienced. Norine tells me she doesn't know how open-minded this priest is, and that before disclosing anything about herself, she has decided to let him talk a little to see what kind of person he is.

'I'm ready to die right now. Death is a transition that will take me to another existence. I don't know why it has to take so much time.

How much longer will I have to be confined to this bed? What's the point?'

She stops suddenly, as if searching for an answer, then continues: 'Perhaps the sacrament of the anointing of the sick will heal me. The priest was due to come today, but he hasn't showed up yet.'

Norine combs her hair, picks an orchid blossom from the plant I've brought her and sets it among her thin white strands in preparation for the approaching visit. She makes me think of my dear grandmother. I tell her, 'You're beautiful, Norine! I'm glad to see you so well cared for in this cosy home.'

'Thank you for coming. This home is bright and clean, but I preferred the hospital, there was more life and more movement. We may not see each other again. Send my greetings to all the hospital staff. Tell them I think of them with gratitude.'

I take Norine's hand and kiss it in farewell.

On my way home, I get stuck in one of the frequent traffic jams on the A411. As I think of Norine's impatience, Marco comes to mind: both of them have a clear sense of the futility of prolonging the wait for the end. 'What's the point?' Norine asked me. But what's the point of *my* life? Is it only the fact of being able to move freely, of being able to read and travel that makes the difference and gives meaning to life? I think that these two old people have come a long way and I'm glad they're still here to teach me to express gratitude, savour friendship, look at the mountains, and detach myself from all material goods. Perhaps the continuation of their lives actually serves to testify to all this.

What's the point of my life? I'm learning not to search for an explanation but to follow my *dharma*, even if it seems to have no value. We are fragments of creation and are not required to do anything extraordinary to experience the presence of the divine in the world, in ourselves, and in the people around us. Often, the smiles of my grandchildren or those of the dying are what make me realize the sense of my life.

Sometimes in the hospital, when waiting for death goes beyond the endurance of the patients and their anguish becomes devastating, they are offered sedation; in other words, a loss of lucidity that may be reversible or persist until death. What is the difference between sedation and euthanasia? Sedation is offered by doctors who know how to accept their limits. There are questions that a doctor cannot answer: 'When will I be released?' Or, 'What's the point of this long agony?' By proposing sedation, doctors free patients from anxiety and accept their own powerlessness.

Sometimes an answer to the question 'What's the point?' arrives mysteriously, as in the case of Anne, a patient whose terminal sedation lasted for over two weeks, beyond the family's capacity to remain with her. This woman was therefore left all alone and everything was removed from her room, including her family photos and anything else that had enhanced it. But one day a granddaughter of about twenty arrived. She came into the room and stayed with Anne for a long time, caressing her and crying. Perhaps it was what Anne had been waiting for because she died the following night.

In contrast to Marco and Norine, there are those who seem in no hurry to die. Jean, the patient in Room 569, is one of these, and has been with us now for a few months. He is a retired professor of formal logic, very old and sick but still lucid. He's a widower and has no children. At times he receives a visit from one of his colleagues or students from the university. He reads, follows international events, and is enthusiastically involved in correcting a doctoral thesis on the design of a 'fuzzy relational database'.

Jean embraces and appreciates the positive side of events that regard him; he is full of gratitude for the care he receives, for the staff's attention and concern, and even for the quality of the hospital food. When we enter his room, he greets us with a smile and kind words. He's learned all our names and remembers everything we've talked about during the long weeks of his hospitalization. He doesn't complain about the pain, but instead expresses his gratitude for the efficacy of the analgesic therapy, which allows him to tolerate the pain while leaving him the clarity of mind that is essential for his intellectual activities. He respects the work of the nurses, whom he tries not to bother with unnecessary calls. If the treatment makes him suffer, he moans in pain, but he tells them not to say anything to the doctors for fear they'll increase the dosage of the analgesics, which might reduce his lucidity.

He has a brain tumour with bone metastases, and a paralysis that confines him to his bed. He is always carefully shaven and wears well-pressed pyjamas and a wig that hides the deformation of his skull, caused by his illness. The salt-and-pepper wig is slightly dishevelled and gives him a youthful, carefree look. When it's too hot and he's not expecting visitors, he takes it off, yet his eyes and his smile still give him a pleasant and attractive appearance. Every now and then he is moved by machine to a chair, but the pains in his legs don't allow him to remain there for more than a couple of hours. He tells me he is checking the PhD thesis of a young scientist friend of his. It's a delicate task because he can't interfere with the responsibility of the supervising professor. The student is very fond of Jean and brings him Prolog programming exercises to keep his brain nimble.

Today, when I brought him lunch, he told me: 'I've never eaten as well as I do in this hospital.' I help him to take his medication and prepare him a chicory coffee, but he's able to eat unaided. I enjoy keeping him company and talking to him.

I don't know much about his medical condition and he's aware of this, which allows him to talk to me about his projects, including those that stem from his completely illusory hopes of a long-term future out of hospital. These are projects he can't talk about to the hospital staff, who know his prognosis only too well. My not-knowing and my mission of no-action become my specialization as a volunteer in the interdisciplinary team; a specialization which, like the innocence of children, brings us close to the hearts of those around us. Jean denies the imminence of his own death and dreams of the unachieved as the 'yet to be achieved': this is his subjective reality at this time, and his right. His desire has to be protected and given value by me as I assist him, because it represents his attempt to live life until the end. The way I look at him has to make him feel that his place is among the living.

After drifting off into a reality that is far from his real prospects as a terminally-ill patient, Jean returns to tell me about his desire to continue his work of completing the supervising of the PhD thesis. Jean teaches me to live in the present and to look with optimism and gratitude on all that I'm still able to do, without regrets for what old age or illness have taken away.

The Son

Léon arrives on the ward accompanied by Winnie, his son. Dr Charles asks me to take care of Winnie while he remains in the room for an initial meeting with Léon. It's a very difficult case and the patient's condition is critical. Léon was admitted to a university hospital where he requested euthanasia. After the examinations and the procedures required by law had all been carried out, the date for the step that would end Léon's life had been set for 30 April. However, the day before, Winnie, his second son, told him in tears that he wanted to assist and accompany him to his natural end. He promised he would remain at his bedside with Hélène, his wife, and that they would never leave him.

Winnie's loving insistence led Léon to change his mind, and when the doctor asked the ritual question, requiring him to confirm his intention to request euthanasia, Léon refused, saying, 'I want to go the natural way, surrounded by my loved ones.'

A few days later, the family realized that Léon had become a cumbersome and unwelcome presence in the hospital, so they decided to transfer him to a small clinic on the outskirts of Brussels where they hoped he would be treated well. But Leon's illness was so complex that the healthcare facility was not able to cope, and therefore the family doctor contacted our service, which could guarantee his admission within a short time.

While Winnie is telling me about Léon's odyssey, Dr Charles leaves the room and we go in with Hélène and their three-year-old-daughter, Agnès, who have arrived in the meantime. Hélène is a young kindergarten teacher; she has asked for the paid leave provided by law so that she can be present with Winnie at her father-in-law's bedside. Winnie goes over to his father and says, 'We'll be fine here. The volunteer who is looking after us told me that we can come and go at any time and also stay the night. His name's Attilio; he must be Italian.'

Then turning to me he says, 'I told Dad that I think you're Italian. I recognize the accent because I often go to Italy for my work.'

Léon turns to look at me. I greet him by telling him that we will take care of him, and he replies weakly, 'Since I've retired, I've sometimes accompanied Winnie on his travels. Last time we were in Bolzano on the wine route.'

Winnie is a wine importer and knows Tuscany, Piedmont and Alto Adige well.

'The wine route is close to my house in Italy,' I tell him. 'I know the Adige valley like the back of my hand and I can give you some advice about the wines worth tasting.'

Talking about the journey they made the previous year during the grape harvest creates a peaceful atmosphere. Meanwhile, Hélène has crouched down beside the bed and is massaging her father-in-law's hands. Agnès, radiant in her white spring dress, explores the room by jumping around the bed. My fourth grandchild — the first girl — is due to be born in a month, and I'm touched at the sight of this little angel running around her dying grandfather's bed, bringing him a message of love, life and happiness.

Agnès goes to her mother to speak in her ear. Hélène asks me, 'Agnès wants to know if she can come and see granddad tomorrow and bring him Puff. Puff is my father-in-law's cat. They're inseparable. When Léon sits in his armchair, Puff is always curled up in a ball next to him, purring constantly.'

'A cat isn't allowed in the hospital for obvious hygienic reasons,' I reply, 'but the wishes of children who love their grandfathers have to be listened to respectfully. I'll see if perhaps in the evening — and with the utmost secrecy — we can make an exception.' Then I say to Agnès, 'To begin with, bring a photo of Puff, and also one of yourself, and we'll stick them on the wall with a magnet next to your grandfather's bed. They'll keep him company and he'll think of you.'

Agnès is satisfied with the proposal. She climbs onto the bed, gives her grandfather a kiss, then gets down and goes running around the room. She stops in front of the balcony window and says hello to the passing cars on the road. A woman is walking along the pavement with a pushchair and a boy of four or five beside it. The boy sees Agnès, who is in full sun behind the window, and responds to her greeting with a wave. 'He saw me!' shouts Agnès.

Léon smiles.

The following afternoon, two photos are on the wall next to the bed: Agnès at the beach with a bucket, and a white, well-groomed Angora cat. Léon is dozing. Every now and then he opens his eyes and sees his loved ones gathered in silence at his bedside.

Léon never woke again. He died in the night in the company of Winnie and his sister Claire. His last look rested on Agnès's photo: the little girl who helped her grandfather to remain alive and happy to the end.

Winnie invited me to the cemetery for his father's burial. Agnès cried in her mother's arms. Later, she wriggled free and began chasing a squirrel that jumped down from a birch, ran gracefully across the lawn, and hid in a hedge of rhododendrons. Hélène said, 'Agnès was crying because Puff is dead too. We found him under Léon's chair. He died the same day as his master.'

Agnès comes back towards her mother smiling, and raises her little hands to be picked up. She says to her, 'Puff's gone to heaven to play hide and seek with granddad.'

First Love

Didier, dean of the volunteers, was born in 1926. He's a widower now and lives alone, but he often spends long periods in Barcelona where his daughter, Éliane, lives with her husband, Paul, and their two boys, now grown. Didier has just returned from a visit to his daughter's home in Spain, and today at the hospital he has the evening shift after me. Before I leave, I spend a little time with him in the kitchen. He tells me about the liveliness of Barcelona, his walks beside the sea with Éliane, and his grandsons' plans as they near the end of their studies. It's obvious that he'd like to live in Barcelona and be close to his daughter's family; perhaps he'd even like to live with them, but he realizes sadly that his visits shouldn't last longer than a few weeks so that he doesn't weigh on them too much, and so that it is clear and evident to everyone, first of all to himself, that his home is elsewhere. If he had the means he'd buy an apartment in Barcelona. He has to think about it: maybe by selling the apartment he has at Saint-Gilles he'd manage it. But that would mean cutting his ties with Belgium, and then what will happen to him when he's no longer autonomous? Here in Brussels there are many services in terms of assistance, housing and care for the elderly. But in Spain?

These reflections occupy us for half an hour. Then I update him on the situation with the patients and give him the list the nurses have prepared containing the patients' names and useful information for our volunteer service.

There are two delicate cases, one of which concerns Rebecca, who after a stay of four weeks is nearing the end of her life. She had been hospitalized in a nursing home as a destitute person receiving public assistance. Written under the heading 'previous residence' in her file was 'no fixed abode'. The social workers found her sleeping in a bed of cardboard at the station. When she came to us from the nursing home she was in a pitiful condition. The doctors' therapy, the competent, assiduous and kindly care of the nurses, the hot baths in the wellness room and the massages from the physio-therapist have transformed her and restored her dignity. The hairdresser has treated her thinning white hair, giving it shape and volume. Despite her grave state of health, Rebecca is now a sick woman who has rediscovered herself.

This is a wonderful result for our service: to restore dignity to a person who had let herself go to the extent of sleeping on the ground at the station, and to treat her like a queen. The volunteers have also played their part in this transformation because no one else ever comes to visit her, nor do we know whom to inform of her presence with us. She is entirely alone; she no longer eats and her slender frame seems to be suspended on the sheets. Today I spent a little time with her in silence. Until last week I helped her to colour the pictures in colouring books, the same ones that my youngest grandchild coloured last year in kindergarten. Her unsteady hand needed to be guided as if she were a small child. She chose the colours but needed help to stay within the outlines of the figures. Today this was too much for her and she has remained resting in her bed. She looked into my eyes and asked me, 'Attilio, is my life still worth something?' Dr Michel Stroobant has taught us that the desire to live or die depends on the relationship the patient has with those who assist them.[23] I caressed her hands and told her that for me and for many on the ward her presence was a profound experience, full of peace and serenity, and that her life was valuable to us because, in giving us her gratitude and affection, she made us feel close to her. I hugged her and promised we would be beside her on her journey; the doctors would continue to work to ensure she didn't suffer, and all the healthcare staff would take care of her so that she would remain beautiful and lovable.

When he reads Rebecca's full name on the list I hand him, Didier gives a start. He checks the date of birth, 31 December 1925, and remains stunned. During the war, Didier was at Malmedy in the Fagnes, staying with his grandparents. A girl of his age called Rebecca lived in the house next door. They met in the playground at school; they played tennis together, and Didier fell in love. Once, in the summer of 1942, they went for a walk in the Val d'Arimont and he held her hand. Perhaps the next day he'd have dared to tell her he loved her. But he never saw her again: her parents left in a great hurry with the whole family, a frequent occurrence for Jews during the war.

Didier never found out where Rebecca had gone, or what had happened to her, and, little by little, he almost forgot her. Not really 'forgot', because sometimes he dreamt of what his life would have been if only he had had the time to tell her how happy he was when he saw her, how thrilling it had been to walk beside her holding her hand, and the secret plan he would have concocted in order to run away with her, away from the war. In the years that followed, even though he met Éveline, whom he had loved with all his heart and who had returned his love, and later Éliane had arrived and they had been happy together, the memory of Rebecca returned every now and then to his heart – often in the morning, when he was still half asleep and he would let himself fall into a dream of Les Fagnes and the green woods of his adolescence. He would linger, imagining he told her he loved her and that he heard a reply that opened a path of hope and love.

'Will it be her?' Didier asks me. 'Will she recognize me? Seventy years have gone by!'

Didier is on tenterhooks, and, as he anxiously draws near to Rebecca's room at the end of the corridor, he asks me to accompany him. The new fittings in the rooms allow the lighting to be dimmed; right now it is very low. I knock on the door and say, 'I'll be coming to say goodbye to you before I go home. The volunteer on duty tonight is called Didier and he's here with me.' Didier goes in, and, not daring to say anything, sits down next to the bed. He stares intently at her and his tears begin to flow. I realize that he has recognized his Rebecca and I leave discreetly.

After a few days I meet Rose, who was on duty that evening. She says that when she went into the room, she saw Didier holding Rebecca's hands in his, and, though both were crying, they bore an air of serenity and bliss. Rose tells me that Didier stayed beside her for a long time. Before going home at the end of her shift, Rose saw him asleep on the chair beside the bed with his head resting on Rebecca's pillow. She woke him and took him home by car.

Didier came back day after day, remaining for long hours next to Rebecca, who now no longer spoke. She let him know every now and then that she was aware of his presence by moving her hand imperceptibly as he caressed it. After four days, Rebecca died peacefully at night.

Didier has gone back to Barcelona. I saw on the Internet that his apartment in Saint-Gilles is for sale.

Live the Present

Desmond, a thirty-five-year-old Irish engineer, arrives on the palliative care ward with his laptop; as did another engineer, Jean-Louis, a sixty-year-old Frenchman, admitted last week.

Desmond is the founder of a consulting company engaged in the installation of heat pumps. He is working on several projects in Switzerland for the 'green' heating of exit ramps for mountain chalet garages. For several months now he has had to slow down the pace of his work due to chemotherapy. He has lung cancer that has recently spread to his pancreas. His condition has deteriorated with a rapidity that the medical team are afraid will prove fatal. He is now hospitalized on the palliative care ward because there are no prospects for his recovery. The development has been so swift that, although Desmond is aware of the seriousness of the situation, he does not fully realize he is reaching the end of his life. Desmond came here with his father, who must be in his sixties and is in excellent health. He is also an engineer and works at a small engineering firm. In recent months he has helped his son, replacing him in managing the work on the construction sites in Switzerland during Desmond's periods of hospitalization.

During his first two days, I spend a lot of time with Desmond, who tells me passionately about his professional work, in particular about the heating for mountain garage ramps. Desmond shows me on his laptop his plans and the photos of his construction sites. He asks me to provide him with a range of information so that he can prepare a plan and proposal for my house in the Dolomites. He has a Belgacom flash drive that allows him to surf the Internet and he shows me with pride the site of the small company of which he is owner, manager and sole member, while Ruby, his partner, is responsible for the accounting, promotion, and secretarial work.

Ruby is about thirty. She's Dutch and, like many Dutch people, speaks several languages well. She comes to visit Desmond regularly in the evening after work. Every now and then I meet her. She speaks to me in English and tells me she is studying Italian. I offer to bring her some good books to read in Italian or audio books to listen to. She accepts and tells me that when she knows Italian well, she'd like to settle in Florence and open a cake shop specializing in Belgian chocolate. Desmond supports this project, proposing that she continue to assist him in his consulting firm part-time, as he dreams about setting up renewable energy home heating projects in Tuscany.

Desmond knows there is no time left for him to move to Tuscany, but he exorcises his fears with this plan, which allows him to imagine himself soon out of hospital. He insists that I bring all the information relating to my home in the mountains.

Jean-Louis, the other engineer, has come from a hospital in Paris. He arrived here accompanied by his daughter, Ohandja, and son-in-law, after an adventurous and difficult journey by car, partly caused by a fuel distributors' strike. In agreement with her two brothers, Ahmadou and Paul, Ohandja decided to move their father to Brussels so that she can keep him company. She lives in Waterloo, where she teaches singing, and will be able to visit him regularly. Her two brothers, however, live respectively in Milan and Yaoundé, Cameroon, Jean-Louis's country of origin.

Jean-Louis has been living in Paris for about thirty years. He's a French citizen and has worked as a consultant for development projects, both in his home country and in other African states. His children all grew up and studied in France. The eldest son, Paul, is twenty-eight and now lives in Yaoundé. He is married and has two beautiful children, whose photos Jean-Louis has shown to the nurses with pride and affection, displaying them on his laptop screen. He shows me a picture of Ahmadou, the youngest son: tall, slim and elegant, who works in the fashion world in Milan. Jean-Louis never speaks to me about the mother of his children. Later I learn from Ohandja that they have been separated for a decade. In Paris, he has a network of professional acquaintances and some dear, close friends, but, given his condition, he decided with his children to spend his last days near to at least one of them. On the other hand, it is important to him to keep in touch with his other two children and with his friends in France. This is why he has brought his laptop. But he is very disappointed by the lack of wi-fi on the ward. I try to resolve this problem by going to buy a USB Internet connection key in a Belgacom shop. This is easier said than done because it is the Christmas holidays and, despite the economic crisis, the stores are packed with people and the reserve supply of electronic products has sold out. However, after half a day of searching, I find one and take it triumphantly to Jean-Louis, but he can't manage to install it. I have to go back to the store with his laptop and this time I return to the hospital with a connection.

Jean-Louis spends many hours writing to his sons and friends, and for an entire afternoon he pretends to forget about the lung cancer with metastases to his bladder and kidneys. The ability to connect to the Internet is a cause for celebration for him, and he expresses his gratitude to me with touching words.

'Since you also live in a country that isn't your own, you can understand better than other people how important it is for me to be in touch today with my loved ones far away. I still need to say some things to my children, my grandchildren and my friends, and feel them close to me at this critical moment. You can't imagine how great the gift is that you've given me, and how much I appreciate your readiness to help. It makes me think of the solidarity in the villages in Africa, and the respect that my people have for the elderly and the dying.'

Today I have time to keep Jean-Louis company. I ask him about his country of origin and his childhood. He tells me that his father encouraged him to study and set aside enough money to provide him, his two brothers and his sister with a university education in France. Before 1960, life was not easy for the African citizens of

French Cameroon. Jean-Louis remembers seeing his father whipped for speaking Bantu instead of French. He himself was whipped twice at primary school for speaking Bantu with a classmate. He tells me that the ban on the local languages has scattered his people's cultural heritage and destroyed traditional medicine, which was based on knowledge transmitted orally from generation to generation. He tells me about the animism and spirituality of his people, mocked and suppressed by European missionaries.

'After having spent your childhood and adolescence in a colonized country, during your thirty years spent in France, how did you overcome the memories of the humiliation you suffered?'

'I have a real reverence for President Ahmadou Ahidjo, who freed my country and formed the Republic of Cameroon, then later unified French and British Cameroon into the Federal Republic of Cameroon. But I also have a sincere appreciation for France, which welcomed me as a migrant, and then, after ten years, gave me French citizenship and assisted my personal and professional growth, allowing me to educate my children in the best schools in the world. The wounds of my youth cannot heal; it would be easier to be cured of the cancer that has spread throughout my body. But I am grateful to France for letting me become integrated and see my children grow up in a democratic and secular country that is overcoming its colonialist policy of the past. I'm also grateful to France and Belgium for the medical care I receive. In Cameroon we haven't yet reached the level of European medical care. If I'd stayed in Yaoundé, I'd probably be long dead by now. Over the years, I've integrated into French society and culture. If you look at my address book on Thunderbird, you'll find more French than Cameroonian correspondents. I think I'm a good French citizen and I contribute through my work as an expert to the national policy of aid to developing countries. I'm very grateful to my father, who encouraged and urged me to study, and at great sacrifice helped me and my brothers and sister to build a better future for our families. I'm also proud of my son, Paul, who after studying in France went to live in Cameroon. My home country needs her best children to return to Africa after completing a good university education in Europe. Paul is an agricultural engineer and lives with his family in Yaoundé. He's got two children. Here, I'll show you their photos,' says Jean-Louis, picking up his precious laptop.

The laptop won't start; the power adapter no longer works. Jean-Louis is like a man drowning in the ocean. I reassure him by telling him that tomorrow I'll bring another one. I offer him a cup of tea and stay a while longer to chat, then I take my leave to spend a moment with Desmond. The nurses have told me that today he's not feeling well.

Desmond is in his freshly made bed, well settled among the pillows. In the last few days he has spent several hours in a chair or at the small table, working on the computer. Today he seems exhausted and has stayed in bed all day.

'I don't feel like talking about work today; let's leave it till tomorrow. Dr Malder has given me some bad news. I can't go home next weekend. I've lost my good mood and my appetite. I just hope that Ruby will visit me soon.'

This morning our team's weekly meeting was held. Charles told us that Desmond's kidney function is impaired. The overall picture is worrying. He warned us that he would tell Desmond that it wouldn't be wise for him to go home for thirty-six hours as was originally intended. I sit next to Desmond in silence. I think of his projects, of Ruby his partner and his young age. He could be my son. After half an hour, Desmond says, 'More than anything else, I'm sorry not to be able to create a family with Ruby and have children with her. She's the woman I always wanted to meet: intelligent, positive and full of energy. I'm thirty-five; it would have been the right moment to get married and start a new life. Now I don't even know if I'll still be here next week. How do I tell Ruby?'

I don't know how to answer Desmond's question. Perhaps the right reply doesn't exist. I let myself be inspired by what comes from deep within me.

'This is the time to tell Ruby of your only certainty: that you love her and would like to be able to make her happy. This is your truth today, and communicating it to Ruby will be the greatest gift you can offer her today. There are days when it's not possible to think about tomorrow and we can only live in the present.'

We remain in silence for a long time, then I say goodbye because I hear Ruby arriving.

Before going to the hospital the next day I buy a power adapter. I take it to Jean-Louis, who greets me gratefully. He asks me to connect the laptop and check that everything is working; then he thanks me and turns it off.

'For now it's enough for me to know that I can use it, yet I feel I need it less and less. But this doesn't mean I don't value your kind help. It's just that I want to share with you an extraordinary experience. A progressive change of perspective is taking place in me about what is essential, important or urgent. It's as if the approach of death is causing me to free myself from being a slave to the urgency that has characterized my profession and conditioned my life. Before the power adapter failed, I received an email from Paul with a picture of his children in front of their home in Yaoundé. I'm glad that the final image I have received is from my homeland.'

This is not the first time that Jean-Louis speaks to me of the imminence of his death. I feel I know a lot about his condition because I participate in the weekly meetings of the team. But he knows it from inside himself, through the mysterious channels that we use to communicate with the source of life. He knows it's no longer the time to expect to be cured and that his journey is coming to an end.

Jean-Louis is tired and closes his eyes. I stay beside him in silence. I think of his life, of the suffering, the sacrifices, the humiliations and his dignity. After a while his breathing becomes calmer and steadier. He has fallen asleep. I leave when Ohandja arrives; she greets me with a questioning gesture and hugs me.

I go to Desmond's room. He's in bed, lying on his left side and looking out of the window. I go to stand by the window so that he sees me and I greet him by name. He replies in a very polite and formal way, 'Good morning. Excuse me, but I don't have the pleasure of knowing you.'

I tell him who I am. I realize that he isn't present in himself. I remain seated for a while beside his bed until he falls asleep. As I leave, I meet his father, who greets me with tears in his eyes and tells me, 'It's terrible how quick the disease is to take him. Dr Malder has advised me not to go away.'

Charles's warning led to Desmond's father remaining in the room for the next few hours, sitting in the chair next to his bed. At the end of the afternoon Ruby arrived. She sat on the bed and took one of Desmond's hands in hers. He half-closed his eyes for a moment, then opened his mouth as if to say something, but what he uttered was unintelligible. His breathing became slower; then, after a gasp, Ruby felt one last vibration of his hand. Ruby turned to Desmond's father, her eyes filled with tears. They remained in silence for a long time, keeping vigil over Desmond until Rose, a nurse of Ruby's age, arrived for a routine check. Ruby has established a good relationship with her and seeing her come in, hugged her, saying, 'It's not fair — you can't die at thirty-five. What will become of me?'

'Let's stay for a while beside Desmond. Then think about who you'd like to be close to you during these days.'

Ruby asks for someone to go home with her so she can choose an outfit for Desmond. Rose calls Nadine, an elderly, efficient and motherly volunteer, who comes to Desmond's room and remains with Ruby and Desmond's father for half an hour, then suggests she accompany Ruby home. Ruby returns to the hospital an hour later with a shirt, a suede jacket, a scarf and corduroy trousers, which she gives to Rose, asking her to care for Desmond as if it were his wedding day.

The next day I spend an hour with Jean-Louis. I'm about to leave for Italy. It's very difficult to say goodbye to a friend when you fear it may be the last time. I have a feeling that this is almost a certainty, given what they have told us in the weekly ward meeting. It's already happened to me that I don't see patients again whom I saw the day before. I'm also learning that even outside the hospital, every meeting could be the last. This helps me to be present, honest and straightforward, also in relationships with my loved ones. Today Jean-Louis is alive; the moment has arrived to fully live the present. We talk about Ohandja and about Paul's sons. When I say goodbye, I tell him I'll be away for three weeks. Embracing me, he says, 'I don't know if I'll still be here when you return. May God protect and be with you.'

After a fortnight, while I'm in Italy, an email informs me of Jean-Louis's death. On my return to Brussels, the nurses give me a letter from Ohandja, written the day before he died, in which she asks me if she owes me anything for buying the power adapter. Above all, she writes kind words and an invitation to call her.

I am glad to be able to speak to her, to offer her my condolences and tell her how important it was for me to have known her father. Ohandja tells me that I can still give him my last respects since the funeral will be held that same day in the afternoon.

His three children and several Cameroonian friends from Paris are at the crematorium. This is the first time I see Ahmadou and Paul. The child to whom Jean-Louis has given the name of the president who liberated Cameroon says to me, in Italian, that he is a fashion model in Milan. He cries as he hugs his sister and brother beside his father's coffin. He has organized the music and staging for a simple and very moving ceremony in memory of his father, a man who has made me understand something profound about the meaning of forgiveness and dignity.

There is another patient in the oncology unit who comes for chemotherapy with his laptop. He wears his eighty years well, and is always carefully dressed. He speaks excellent French, but with a slight British accent. His name is Jack, and every three weeks on a

Wednesday he spends all his therapy time writing on his laptop. One time, while bringing him a cup of tea, I ask him what he's working on with such passion.

'I'm proofreading the draft of a book,' he tells me. I tell him that I also spend some of my time writing, and I ask him what his book is about.

'It concerns my experiences at work many years ago. I've been retired for thirty-five years, and now that certain documents have been declassified, I can tell about my activities in the British Secret Intelligence Service, the department that was known by the abbreviation MI6 during the Cold War. I worked in counterintelligence and I hope that my memoirs will be as exciting as Ian Fleming's novels, with the difference that in my case they deal with true stories and verifiable events. It's a case of saying that reality surpasses the imagination.'

Jack has been married for forty-five years to Lydia, a seventy-year-old woman who always sits next to him, but without distracting him from his activities. She is immersed in reading James Joyce, but every so often she looks affectionately at Jack and checks that the drip is working properly. She has established a very good relationship with the nurses, who practise their English with her, certain of being corrected with kindness if they make a mistake with a word or a pronunciation. Lydia believes, perhaps rightly, that the tea we offer them is not up to the expectations of two British subjects and goes to prepare it for Jack and herself in the ward's kitchenette. She says she loves the Mediterranean cuisine and, perhaps to make up for the obsession with tea, she admits that the pasta she makes is overcooked compared with orthodox Italian spaghetti.

I suggest that she come with her husband to my home for dinner one evening during the week, before the next chemotherapy, when Jack will be on good form. I promise her there'll be *melanzane alla parmigiana*.

I hadn't expected to meet a '007' in hospital. The variety of human experience that emerges from the relationship with patients always manages to surprise me. In my own field of work, I was used to only meeting people from the same social class, with whom I shared natural affinities and common interests. I'm discovering that the world is larger and richer than the one in which I've lived since I left school. I'm fascinated by this larger sample of humanity that my new role brings me into contact with. This experience suggests to me that the real problems of life are basically always the same, regardless of the profession or status of the individual. At the end of the day, the only thing that matters is the richness and depth of the relationships we establish with the people around us. This is what gives meaning to our lives; it is what will remain of us after our death and what our loved ones will always carry in their hearts.

The Butcher

Alex has an impressive physique; once he must have been as strong as a bull. His pronounced facial features are softened by thick white hair that emphasizes the blue of his eyes, while his mouth is so big that the teeth are separated by large gaps. His giant features are in great contrast to his very obvious and extreme weakness. Besides the cancer that is taking his life, Alex is suffering from acromegaly, a rare disease that causes the abnormal growth of certain body parts, in his case the face and hands. It can also lead to various forms of heart disease and metabolic disorders. Alex has told me that he used to be a butcher and that for a time he ran a butcher's shop in Anderlecht, on the Chaussée de Mons, in front of a large garage. He lived with his wife in an apartment on the first floor above the shop.

After a few days we got to know each other well, and once he told me sadly, 'I'll soon be gone and I feel I've done nothing good with my life — to start with, I haven't been able to have children.'

I answered him, 'I don't believe that among your memories there aren't some special moments or episodes that you can recall with pride. Think things over and I'm sure that later you'll remember something good that you can tell me about. Meanwhile, I'm going to make coffee for a patient who's asked me for a cup, and then I'll be back. I'll bring a cup for you, too, if you like.'

When I return to his room half an hour later, he greets me with a broad smile that displays the gaps between his top teeth.

'I've remembered something good. Stay and listen and I'll tell you the story.

'A long time ago (maybe that's why it didn't come to mind earlier), while I was at the counter slicing beef, I heard screams, gunshots and shouting in the street. On the other side of the road opposite the butcher's, I saw people lying on the ground, while a madman with a gun in his hand was trying to open the rear door of a car parked crosswise in front of a garage. I could see him from behind, standing in the road on the left side of the car, almost in front of my shop. Without thinking twice, I grabbed the knife I used for cutting up young bullocks, ran out into the street and pointed the weapon against the villain's back quickly enough to take him by surprise. As the blade cut through his clothes and began to enter between his ribs, I shouted, "Throw down the gun or you're dead! I'm used to cutting up pigs!" The man dropped the gun on the ground and raised his hands. Meanwhile, my wife, who was at the till in the shop, had called the police. When she saw the madman had been disarmed, she came out into the street and went over to the car where the two women were lying on the ground, one on each side, and both apparently dead. Two children were crying on the back seat. Agnes had them get out on the pavement side of the car, took the smaller one in her arms, the other one by the hand, and brought them up to our apartment. A police car arrived at the scene shortly afterwards.

'The police took charge of the criminal I'd disarmed and drove him away in handcuffs. I was made to get into a second car and they took me off to the police station, still with the knife in my hand and wearing my butcher's apron. As we were leaving, I saw two ambulances arrive, but one would have been enough: the mother of the two children was already dead.'

Alex's story refers to a crime that caused a sensation more than twenty years ago: one that I recall vividly because the woman who survived is Colette, the wife of a colleague of mine. She's a civil lawyer, and that day she'd gone with her friend to collect the friend's children from school before they all returned home to spend some time together. The murdered woman was the wife of the garage manager and they lived above the garage. The murderer was an ex-partner of the manager who believed he'd been wrongly treated; he had therefore decided to take the law into his own hands by killing his ex-partner's family.

Alex says with a smile, 'I haven't always been a saint, but that day I think I did what I had to do and so saved the lives of two children who would otherwise have been victims of the murderous rage that killed their mother.'

Alex is moved by the memory of this act of courage and continues to tell me more. He leans towards me where I'm sitting next to his bed, listening enthralled to his memories.

'I've already had my reward,' he goes on, lowering his voice as if to tell me a secret. 'I have to tell you that now and again I did a bit of cheating. I took a night school course in electrical engineering and used what I'd learned there to devise a system of fixing the scales so that the weight increased if I pressed a pedal under the counter. The scales seemed perfectly correct when inspected by the authorities, but if I saw a customer who was distracted, or one I thought would pay without question, or perhaps a man sent shopping by his wife who was bit out of his depth, I pressed the pedal and the trick was done. This worked for a while and helped to round up the family budget, but in the end the fraud was discovered, my licence was revoked for six months, and the shop was closed. I couldn't pay the rent for the apartment or for the shop and found myself summoned by the Justice of the Peace without even having the money to pay a lawyer. The owner of the building requested the seizure of the furniture in my house and the expensive shop equipment. I was done for. But to my surprise, at the hearing the owner proposed a settlement where the charges would be dropped against me, and the dispute would end with terms favourable to me. I couldn't believe my ears! The proposed solution not only gave me more time to pay, but also I'd be able to honour the debt since the suspension of the licence was to be revoked. I'd be able to manage it; I could start working again. Only later did I learn that the woman who'd survived the shooting was the owner's lawyer. She'd remembered me when she was studying the case, and convinced her client to offer a solution I could satisfy. Now I can't even remember her name, but if I met her again, I'd give her a hug.'

'You see, Alex, not only have you got your heroic action to be proud of, but you've also received special recognition for it.'

Alex is emotional and tired from his long account. I remain with him in silence until I see he has dozed off.

As soon as I get home, I phone Colette and say, 'Do you remember Alex, the butcher of Chaussée de Mons? I met him at the hospital where he's dying. He remembers you as a person linked to a heroic moment in his life. If you can, go and see him; you'd be giving him an enormous gift. The fact is, he's been left alone because his wife, Agnes, died a couple of years ago and, as perhaps you know, they couldn't have children.'

Two days later, I return to the hospital and go to see Alex.

'You can't imagine who came to see me — no one less than the lady who survived the shooting. She said it was you who told her I was in hospital. Seeing her made me cry for joy and I finally got to thank her for what she did for me in court. She replied that it was she who had to thank me. She also told me that her poor friend's children, who must be almost thirty by now, had been brought up by their father and grandparents. She said that they are also alive due to me.'

Alex is in seventh heaven. Colette's visit has restored his self-esteem and pride in his past.

A week later, Alex's condition worsens because of cardiac complications due to diabetes, which in turn is a consequence of acromegaly. He is slipping away serenely. He can no longer speak but still communicates with his eyes. I sit next to him and take one of his great hands in mine. I look at him affectionately and in his blue eyes I see him answering me: there's a secret I share with this gentle giant. I've made enquiries about the two children he saved. I tell him that Jean, the elder, is now twenty-nine years old and, after graduating in mechanical engineering from the Free University of Brussels, works in Tychy, Poland, in a Fiat factory. He'd begun by using the spanners in his father's garage and is now a young manager in a large factory that is the pride of the Polish workers.

Alex listens tranquilly. He hadn't been able to have the children he'd wanted with his wife, but what Colette has told him allows him to think of Jean with paternal affection. I tell him that Jean is also his son: he is alive thanks to his courage and generosity. I think Alex understands me because his large hand trembles between mine, while the last tears shine in his blue eyes.

The Granddaughter

Two weeks ago Rose gave me a warm welcome when I returned to the department of palliative care; I'd been absent for a few months for health reasons.

Rose gives me a list of patients, plus information that will help me in my work. None of the patients whom I'd assisted back in April are still here. Next to the name of one of the new patients, Tatiana in room 437, it says 'speaks Russian'. I ask Rose, 'Do you mean that Tatiana only speaks Russian?'

Rose answers me smiling, 'Da. Until the 1980s Tatiana was an advisor at the Belgian Soviet Embassy and they told me that back then she was fluent in English, French and Arabic. Over the last years, due to age, leukaemia, various cerebral haemorrhages and all the treatments she's had, she's lost part of her mental faculties and only Russian remains, though I have noticed that sometimes she understands French if I speak slowly and enunciate the words carefully.'

I do my rounds and after a few hours arrive at room 437. I ask if I can come in and introduce myself. In front of me, sitting in an armchair, is a tiny lady of about eighty in a dressing gown. She has a slender build and can't be very tall. Her large round head, framed by thick white hair, brings to mind the Mouth of Truth at the church of Santa Maria in Cosmedin in Rome. I sit next to her and begin to talk to her slowly in French, enunciating the words clearly as Rose advised me. Every now and then Tatiana looks at me, but without showing any sign of really seeing me. She's peaceful, but absent. I bring her tea with *Speculoos* biscuits. She says to me, 'No càfe, chaj.'

'Yes,' I say, 'it's tea.'

Tatiana tastes it and makes a gesture with her head as if to say 'that's enough'. She says something to me that I don't understand, but it sounds like 'Gieona?'.

I continue talking to her, telling her I know that, years ago, she worked just a short walk from where we are now, and that if she looks out from the balcony, she might recognize the avenue where her embassy is located. But there's no way of reaching her. Every so often she repeats 'Gieona?'. I need to find a means of communicating with her.

When I get home, I call Giorgio, a translator at the European Commission, and ask him if we can meet. When we do, I begin by asking him what 'Gieona?' means. He explains that it's probably *Gdje ona?*, or 'Where is she?'. Tatiana wants to know where a certain woman is. It's a starting point.

I ask Giorgio how to say a few simple sentences in Russian, such as 'I've come back to see you', 'Would you like some tea?', or 'Would you like to sit in the armchair?', and in this way I equip myself with a series of phrases I learn by heart. On my next shift in the hospital, these phrases, combined with my uncertain pronunciation, surprise and amuse Tatiana, but ultimately this stratagem I've devised is counterproductive and frustrating because Tatiana answers me, imagining that I understand what she says, whereas I'm unable to go any further in communicating with her. Therefore I change strategy and return at once to Giorgio to ask him how to say in Russian: 'How do you say this in Russian?', while I point at things with my finger.

In this way, the next day I am able to communicate with Tatiana and I learn how to say *chair*, *window*, *pillow*, *bedcover* and *glass* in Russian. Repeating the words and correcting my pronunciation keeps us busy for some time and helps to establish a relationship. Then Tatiana asks again, 'Where is she?'

Last Monday, Galina, a social worker from the Russian Federation Embassy, came to visit Tatiana. I took the opportunity to have Galina tell me something about Tatiana. She retired in 1986 and decided to remain in Brussels, the last posting in her brilliant diplomatic career. Already a widow for ten years, she was living alone because her two children had stayed on in the United States, where they'd lived with their parents during their college years. Tatiana has hardly any relationship with them now; the only person who is close to her is Liudmila, a granddaughter of thirty who lives in Athens. Tatiana has asked the social worker to inform Liudmila about her condition and to beg her to come and hug her grandmother before it's too late. Liudmila has understood that time is running out and has promised Galina that she'll try to come as soon as possible, even though she has difficulties in buying a plane ticket because her salary as a nurse's aide has been drastically reduced.

Today I'm back on the ward and I spend a little time in Tatiana's room. The doctor said in our weekly meeting that her general condition has deteriorated and that she is close to the end. At the moment she's in bed, but she's not resting. Her expression is lost and absent. I sit next to her on the window side and stroke her right arm. Every now and then she looks at me and whispers again, 'Where is she?'

I tell her in French that Liudmila spoke with Galina, that she is thinking of her and will come and visit. I repeat this again, pronouncing the words carefully. When I say Liudmila's name, for a moment Tatiana's eyes light up. I remain in silence a while longer, then, when I see she's asleep, I move away and continue my round of the ward.

In Chantal's room at the end of the corridor, I find the haughty, elegant woman who lives on the first floor of my own apartment building. It's the first time that we encounter each other in the hospital and I learn that Chantal is her mother, whom she's come to visit. She's very surprised to see me there in my hospital tunic and, in her amazement at finding me in any setting other than the apartment owners' annual meeting, she asks me: 'Mr Stajano, what are you doing here?'

I explain my role and tell her that recently I had an intense visit with Chantal, whom I did not know was her mother because she is registered under her maiden name.

'That's wonderful!' she replies, 'I'm glad my mother is being assisted so well. And by the way, I have a good friend on the board of this hospital. I could get you an excellent recommendation.'

I thank her, declining her offer, and suggest that I'll return to her mother when she's alone again.

On my way back, I pass room 437 again. The door is open and I see that Tatiana is in the armchair and that she is not alone. I enter discreetly. A young woman, beautiful and smiling, is sitting next to her, holding Tatiana's hand between her own and speaking in her language. Tatiana is staring into her eyes but she glances away for a moment to welcome me and makes a gesture that says, 'She came; she came for me!'

Tatiana is transfigured. Her face is suffused with happiness and her eyes shine through a veil of tears. She smiles and shakes her head from side to side as if to say that none of this seems possible. Her granddaughter strokes her, then embraces her and cries with her.

I walk away on tiptoe. I think of everything that Tatiana has left behind and from which she has progressively detached herself: her native country, her husband, her children, her status as an embassy advisor, later her health and, finally, her lucidity. But today she is happy because Liudmila, through the warmth of her affection, has brought with her a ray of sunshine. Liudmila's presence allows Tatiana to shed tears of happiness and love.

Rose is on duty today, too. When I see her leave room 437 I go up to her and say, 'Have you seen the happy reunion?'

Rose is as moved as I am and replies, 'Tatiana's happiness is the culmination of her whole life. She's understood where the greatest treasure is to be found, and in dying teaches us how to live.'

A Friend

It has been a couple of years since I've visited Pio, an eighty-five-year-old Jesuit priest whom I originally met when he was the young chaplain at the University La Sapienza in Rome and I was still a student. Now, as I'm writing the chapter 'They Still Have Something To Tell Us', I receive a phone call from Domenico, a nurse in Rome who's a friend of mine, though I haven't seen him for ten years. He tells me that Pio is dying and is asking for me. Pio is more than a friend: he was my mentor for many years. We continued seeing each other regularly even when I left his spiritual path, and I have always found him open, ready to help, and respectful. In 2009, the last time we met, Pio was studying the *Bhagavad Gita* and spoke passionately to me about the spiritual experience in India of one of his fellow brothers.

In the 1960s, students arriving in Rome from other provinces found very little student housing or university residences available and the rental market was already in the hands of speculators. In a working-class neighbourhood near the university, Pio managed to create a kind of student house that welcomed young students from various backgrounds and extractions who were living away from home. Discreet and effective fundraising allowed him to also provide accommodation for students with limited financial resources, making up for the inefficiency and inadequacy of the institutions. For fifty years he has offered a multidisciplinary and intellectually-stimulating environment for students during the course of their university education, thus allowing thousands of young people to develop and grow in a spirit of sharing and openness.

For many years, when my work took me to Rome for a few days, I often went to visit him, taking part in the lively intellectual and political evening activities that the students organized, which also included many of the people who had lived there previously during their university years. Over the years, an informal group developed, made up of men and women of all ages and professions, whose diverse positions, experiences and beliefs were united by the spirit of consideration and respect for the ideas of others that this priest was able to instil.

I am touched and honoured that Pio is asking for me. Domenico, the young nurse, tells me that, although Pio is still conscious, the end is imminent and his condition might quickly worsen. I have guests at home who've come a long way to visit me, but I drop everything and everyone and leave immediately for Rome.

Pio is in the Sandro Pertini hospital, a relatively new building near the large Rebibbia prison. There is a ward for prisoners in the hospital; ambulance sirens mingle with those of the prison service. Pio is in a room with four beds on the internal medicine ward. One of the other patients is a forty-year-old businessman, admitted for a series of clinical tests. He spends his time on the phone talking with customers and suppliers. Another is an old builder who is dying; he complains in dialect, insulting the nurse who administers the pre-scribed treatment. The third has just arrived and seems to be deeply asleep.

Domenico explains to me that there is no palliative care ward for the terminally ill at the Pertini, and, indeed, that there are none in any of the other Rome hospitals either.[24]

Pio wants to die in his own home, and his friends are making arrangements to take him back there in a few days' time.

When I arrive, Pio is asleep and lying sideways. The head of the bed is raised, but he has slipped down and can't breathe well. His extremely emaciated left arm is outside the covers, attached to a drip administering a transfusion. Domenico makes him more comfortable with the sure gestures of a professional, and the deli-cacy that affection and devotion ordain towards the very man who many years ago assisted Domenico's own father until he died, and who then helped him during his years of study. Domenico

('Mimmo' to friends, whom I'm honoured to be among) told me on the way to the hospital that Pio's haemoglobin level is extremely low, and that in the last two days he's received four transfusions in order to restore him to a sufficiently stable state to return home. The cancer has now reached his spinal cord and the effect of these transfusions will be short-lived, but at least it will give him the strength to bear the move back to his apartment, which from time immemorial he has shared with students and young workers.

I sit next to him and think of the many experiences we've shared. I'm glad I've arrived in time. It's a Saturday afternoon before visiting hours begin; Mimmo has let me visit early. My thoughts are interrupted by the businessman's constant phone calls and the builder's vulgar complaints. I think Pio is happy not to be in a single room and instead to be treated like any other patient, despite the clumsy attempts of his Order and a number of friends — well-known doctors — who have brought pressure to bear for him to receive special treatment.

After some time, Pio opens his eyes, sees me and recognizes me.

'So you came,' he says.

I hug him, very moved, and tell him that I'm glad he thought of me and am grateful that he let me know about his condition.

'As soon as I heard you were ill I rushed to Rome. I'm here now to answer your call, to tell you I love you, and to be near to you at this time. You look thinner, but I'm glad to see you're tidy and shaved to perfection.'

Pio tells me that Francesco, a mutual old friend, came by this morning and shaved him.

'They keep me company all the time, but in spite of that, this is not the place where I want to die. I want to go back to my boys, keep working, and die at home.'

I reassure him, telling him that Mimmo and other friends are busy organizing his return home within two or three days, the time required to prepare his room with a hospital bed and set up home care. This seems to calm him, allowing him a moment of rest, from which he wakes after half an hour. He talks to me, confusing me with Raniero La Valle, another friend of his from the 1950s and '60s. I'm honoured that Pio links and confuses me with Raniero, a committed left-wing Catholic journalist who publicized the achievements of the Second Vatican Council and countered the conservative forces in the Curia. We recall that heroic period, full of hopes and expectations, the outcome of the innovative ideas of Pope John XXIII. Suddenly, like a Fury, a little nun bursts into the room and, so excited she can hardly breathe, says: 'I knew it! I realised! You're Father Pio Parisi. You preached a spiritual retreat in 1985 at my convent in Cosenza. I'm Sister Giuseppa from Reggio Calabria, from the Congregation of the Sisters of Charity of SS Bartolomea Capitanio and Vincenza Gerosa — the ones known as the Sisters of Maria Bambina. I've never forgotten your sermon. We spent a whole week in silence! What a penance! Now I'll pray with my fellow-sisters for your full and speedy recovery.'

Pio looks at her as if to say that in this case he hopes her prayers will not be answered. While waiting for her chatter to subside, he closes his eyes to rest. In the meantime, visiting hours have begun and the whole ward has come alive like a supermarket. Pio sleeps. Lino, Pio's GP, arrives. Lino is also an ex-*appartamentista* — the neologism we coined for the tenants of the student apartments that Pio manages. I talk with Lino about Pio's condition and his decision to die at home. He tells me that he's in contact with a palliative care service that will ensure the details of Pio's home care in terms of medical treatment, nursing and insurance. He tells me that Pio was admitted to the Pertini six days earlier for a series of tests, and that the oncologists decided not to subject him to other therapies, given that improvement is no longer possible. To his mind, the transfusions prescribed are superfluous, and, in any case, the one presently taking place will be the last. It should ensure his safe transfer home in the coming days.

Coordinating assistance for Pio is in the hands of Pino, another loyal friend. He is organizing the schedule for Pio's friends to assist him during his hospital stay. I express my availability and agree to spend a part of Sunday night with him. I'll take over from Liborio on Monday morning at 1 o'clock and stay until 9 o'clock, after which, for a couple of hours, friends and family are not allowed. Now it's late Saturday afternoon and there's an uninterrupted stream of visitors. There are many for Pio, among whom a number of old acquaintances of mine whom I greet with feeling.

I leave, and return on Sunday morning at 11 o'clock, when I'm the only visitor in Pio's room. I sit quietly beside him. He looks exhausted and absent, very different from his condition yesterday. I gently take one of his hands in mine and in his eyes I read a sign of greeting. We remain in silence for a long time. Three women arrive, one about thirty and two who are very old. They look at some papers and say, 'Two patients here have requested the Eucharist.'

On saying this, they turn to the patient next to Pio, who was asleep yesterday too. They call him softly by name, but he doesn't answer and the young businessman tells them that he's a newly arrived patient. The pious women don't lose heart, however, and turn to Pio in his abandoned and absent state. They begin to read the Gospel of the day, Matthew 17, on the transfiguration of Jesus. They then recite together: 'I confess to almighty God, to the Blessed Mary [...] that I have greatly sinned, in my thoughts and in my words, in what I have done and in what I have failed to do...'

Pio has his eyes closed and shows no sign of hearing them. The women consult and decide to give him the consecrated host, which they carry in a small pyx. They put one in his mouth and then become afraid that he won't be able to swallow it. They discuss amongst themselves what to do. Pio half closes his eyes and seems to beg to be left in peace. The pious women linger, twittering various prayers until they believe that Pio has swallowed the host; then, with various signs of the cross, they leave to go to the next room, where, once again, they recite the Gospel for the day.

I think of a Sunday in spring more than fifty years ago when Pio read and commented on that same passage. I was twenty and madly in love with a girl who was studying modern literature. I remember Pio said that just as a young man in love sees his partner transfigured by the experience of love, and through it, grasps the true, deep and mysterious nature of the woman who loves him, so Peter, James and John are surprised, rejoice, and are deeply moved by understanding in Jesus the true nature of Christ: not the triumphant, armed and powerful Christ who will free Israel from the yoke of Rome, but the Messiah united to the Father, the personification of forgiveness, love and freedom. The memory of that Sunday reopens an old wound. In that distant spring I had dared not go against my father, who had ordered me to give up the girl and our plans for our love. This betrayal has tormented me all my life. I would like to talk to Pio about the passage from Matthew, the girl, our memories and my remorse, but I realize that his condition won't allow it today, and perhaps never will again. So I remain quietly beside him as he sleeps. Soon he will enter into the joy of his Lord, who will welcome him and show him his face, recalling all the occasions in which Pio has acknowledged the presence of Christ in the lowly and the poor, and enumerating all the experiences and acts of his life that were animated by the divine spirit of love. Among these is the deep and true friendship that binds us. I become lost in contemplating the mystery of that part of me that is in him, which through him and through his death will be presented to the Father. I get a jolt when a nurse briskly invites me to leave, announcing the visit of the doctor on duty. I embrace Pio and withdraw.

When I return to the hospital, Liborio, another former student a little younger than me, is at his bedside. Pio is asleep. Liborio accompanies me into the corridor and tells me that in the dark, shortly before, Pio had confused him with me, talking about my home in Brussels, which he'd visited years ago. Liborio tells me that Pio is disturbed and restless, then he re-enters to say goodbye to him before leaving. Next to the bed there's an armchair and a chair. I settle myself on the chair to be closer to him and to avoid the risk of falling asleep. I whisper to him, 'It's Attilio, I'll be with you tonight. I hope you rest,' so that he understands I'm there and that I'll stay beside him in silence. I don't have any plan for tonight; it's enough for me to be present. I only hope there'll be a moment when I can have a talk with my friend. I'm used to spending long hours next to patients who are drowsing or comatose. It's a very intense experience during which I have the impression of being in touch with them. This particular night, the closeness to this dying man brings back many emotional memories. I think of another priest whom I watched over in Pisa forty years ago. His name was Renzo. He was my parish priest and was in a critical condition after a fall while climbing the Apuan Alps. He had multiple fractures that, among other things, had pierced his lungs. He managed to survive and, after six weeks of hospitalization, during which he never once rang the bell, he was discharged, though he still needed a long period of convalescence before he could return to his church. Thirty years later, I dreamt of him one night and had the desire to see him again. A couple of weeks later, taking advantage of a trip to Italy, I went to his rectory in Pisa. The door was locked. When I rang, a small window opened, high up on the fourth floor, like in the story of Pinocchio. A little priest looked out and I asked after Father Renzo. He replied from the window without any kind of preamble, 'He died a fortnight ago.' And with that, the little window promptly closed.

With Pio it will be different: we have the whole night ahead of us. He is absent and helpless, resting without sleeping. He becomes agitated, asks to be moved, requests a sip of water. Every now and then he has a moment of clarity. He asks me about my children and my life. I tell him about my work as a volunteer at the hospital and this leads us to talk about death. Pio tells me he would like to return as soon as possible to his apartment and resume his work, continuing until the end. It seems to me that for him, death is like an accident along a continuous path. I think of the young *appartamentisti* living with him. They'll have an experience of death lived in silence, diligence, communication and friendship.

I tell him, 'You've given us and still give us an example of loyalty, integrity and consistency. To us, your friends, you represent the reconstruction of a church founded on the Word that returns to its origins, that shuns power and embraces the lowly. I see a host of young and not so young people who have received this message. You can say, like Paul, that you've fought to the end. You've finished the race and you've remained faithful.'

We talk about his distant memories, such as when, as a small child, his parents took him on holiday to Lipari, where he collected the pumice stones that were floating in the sea. He brought them back to Rome, and when his mother washed him he put them in the bathtub and played with those unsinkable ships. Then he tells me of a holiday in Canazei in the 1930s, his passion for the mountains, and a trip to the Viel del Pan trail that faces the Marmolada glacier — a trip that was tough for a child in those days when there were none of the lifts that now reach the Belvedere in minutes. These memories emerge gradually, between a moment of deep sleep and one of wakefulness. I ask him what his most precious memory is. He doesn't answer me and I think he's dozed off. Instead he's thinking and he replies after a long silence.

'I was thirty years old, newly ordained, and I was asked to go on a mission. It was a difficult prospect — somewhat heroic and certainly fascinating. After much deliberation I chose to stay in Rome. I believed that it would be here in Rome that I'd meet the real challenges and the greatest difficulties. I don't think I was wrong and I don't regret my choice.'

When Pio tells me this, it reflects the coherence his life has had, his social commitment, his marginalization within the Jesuit order, and his protection of the weak and the poor. I wonder if the calm manner in which he is approaching death is because he is a priest. But I believe that it is not the sole source of his serenity. I've known many patients who do not profess to be believers and who face the end of life with great serenity. I think that what really counts is to have expressed the feelings of friendship, love and forgiveness that have illuminated our lives, and when we are removed from all that has burdened and muddled us, to recognize that we are not indispensible, knowing that what we leave behind as 'yeast' for our community (Pio would call it 'the prophecy'), will be taken up by others who will know how to continue our journey better than we could do. I remember he once wrote: 'Let's try not to fall into the trap of exalting a priest [...] "now he really *is* a good Christian!" while ignoring, perhaps without realizing it, that so many others are too.'[25]

I remain for some hours in the silence of the night, broken only by the far away blare of the ambulance sirens. The noise stops once they enter the hospital area and silently arrive at the casualty department next to our pavilion. I think of all the health workers and military police who watch over our health and safety every night. When I'm in Brussels and I read the international and Italian papers, I have the impression that in Italy nothing works at all, and that nothing ever will. Then, when I come to Italy, I note that when I press a switch, surprisingly, the light comes on, and that the country is populated by industrious, creative people – and to some extent, happy ones – who carry on living in an orderly chaos, making a cheerful effort to get by, despite an incompetent, dissolute and corrupt administration.

Pio wakes from his doze. I ask him if he thinks that he's left his work in good hands, ensuring its continuation when he can no longer take care of it. He tells me that Antonio, his doctor's brother, will take over responsibility for it. Pio is certain he's made a good choice. More hours pass. Outside the window, the silhouettes of the trees are becoming visible. Pio asks me, 'What is first light called? Sunrise or dawn?'

I remind him that dawn is the first light at the end of the night, before the rising of the sun. I tell him that the sun is about to rise on the first day of spring. He replies: 'Life will move forward into another season. I hope to return home today and to be able to continue to write, work, pray and reflect.'

This old priest who is dying is still looking forward as if he were only thirty. I recall the antiphon he used to recite at the beginning of the Mass, when he was the chaplain at the University of Rome before the Second Vatican Council: *Introibo ad altare Dei, ad Deum qui lætificat Juventutem meam* [And I will go into the altar of God, to God who giveth joy to my youth].

Pio returned home that same day and lived another six weeks. As far as his remaining energy allowed, he continued to work with his 'boys', trying to interpret the Scriptures and to reflect on his spiritual testament,[26] which still today, encourages and challenges us. One phrase of his echoes in me: 'God speaks to each of us; everyone is in some way the Word of God. In this we are all prophets, through whom God speaks. We may be consciously aware of this or not. The prophecy is not what we think and communicate, but what God communicates to us, and which in many different ways we transmit to others.'

Pio's journey towards death reminds me of a past event. When I was about ten years old, I attended the oratory of a church in via Piemonte in Rome. During the interval in a football game, a priest told us a story that I later found in a book by Guy Gilbert.[27] St Giovanni Bosco asked the very young Domenico Savio, who was busy playing football, 'What would you do if you knew that in a few hours you were going to die?'

And Domenico replied, 'I'd go on playing.'

The Family Doctor

Inge, my partner, lost her fight against cancer. Almost thirty years have gone by since then, but I remember it as if it were yesterday...

The consultant oncologist at the Bordet Institute calls me into his office to tell me that he plans to stop the chemotherapy unless I think it better to continue with a placebo so that she won't immediately realize that the end is imminent.

It is Guy, our family doctor, who tells her. I am also present, together with Solange, a psychologist at the Association Cancer et Psychologie, who has been assisting us for several months. Guy tells Inge that the doctors here at the Bordet Institute can try nothing further to cure her and have suggested discontinuing the chemotherapy and limiting treatment to relieving the pain, assuring her of their assistance to the end. Inge has been expecting the news and says that under the circumstances she'd prefer to go home.

It is the last stage in a long ordeal. Only eight months ago there was talk of a strong probability of recovery. Then, after a first operation, given the extent of the metastases it became a question of assessing the chances of survival. Four months later there was an unexpected improvement, but then other complications set in and the doctors made me take another step back along the path of hope when they began to doubt whether to continue therapy.

These eight extremely difficult months have been a devastatingly intense experience, but one that has enabled us to discover the power of love and friendship. Now we know that our projects and dreams will never be realized. So Inge has asked to end her life at home, in the house that we lovingly furnished with the idea of living there happily for years.

I tell the senior consultant of her decision; he is against it and puts me on my guard, explaining that she might need treatment that can only be performed safely in hospital. He also informs me that his team is not able to assist people at home, and, in the event of an emergency, he could only assist if Inge were readmitted. However, he leaves me free to decide what to do, advising me that if I am determined to bring Inge home, to find a qualified doctor with unconditional availability.

I do not lose heart and go to see the gynaecologist that Inge has had for many years. He is dismayed, but tells me he is not able to provide home care. So then I go to see Guy, who has been my family doctor for ten years. It takes a good half hour to get there from home by car. This has never been a problem since I've only needed to see him once or twice a year. However, we now have to ask him to visit, and probably often.

Guy is my age and has taken our case to heart, advising and assisting us step by step up until now. When cancer was diagnosed, Inge and I did not expect it at all and I felt completely unprepared for such a cruel test. I decided to enrol for a weekend seminar on dying, conducted by a renowned psychoanalyst and intended for health professionals and the family members of patients who were dying. On the Saturday morning that I arrived for the first seminar meeting, I was surprised to find Guy there. I went over to greet him and he said, 'I need help to accept Inge's diagnosis and to assist you at this difficult time.'

I was deeply touched and hugged him. I knew then that I would not be alone to face the disease, or the uncertainties and challenges that it would bring.

Today Guy reassures me. He doesn't conceal the difficulties there will be in terms of caring for Inge out of hospital, but he thinks he can manage because the palliative care home service will help us, and therefore there shouldn't be a frequent need for him. I can also count on various friends who have already demonstrated their availability and support. I feel that we will manage.

Now it's time to organize the return home. The social worker offers me her help in arranging all the practical and insurance issues, and explains to me all the steps that need to be taken to ensure the regular presence of doctors, nurses and physiotherapists according to the programme developed by Continuing Care,[28] a palliative home care organization.

It takes a few days to equip our house and to set up the home care. Guy is in contact with the doctors at the hospital and the two doctors from Continuing Care. I make the house welcoming, as if for a bride returning from her honeymoon. Everything is ready and an ambulance brings Inge home. The nurses at the hospital say a warm goodbye, and Rita promises Inge she will come by on her next day off.

Inge is happy to be home. It's a sunny day and the house is warm and full of light. She finds her favourite yellow roses in her room and a bed like the one in hospital. She's tired, but she smiles at me and calls me to her to hug me. Then she asks me to lower the blinds in the hope of being able to rest. Reassured to find herself back in her own environment, she falls asleep serenely.

I'm alone with her in the house. I can count on a dozen close friends who are willing to take turns in keeping her company and helping her. I prepare a message in which I say that we have come home and ask them when they could be available over the next fortnight in order to arrange shifts that will allow me to leave the house when necessary and continue to work. I know Béate will be here soon. I make a list of things to buy or get hold of that the circumstances require. I order a dozen copies of the keys to our house, which in the coming days will be enlivened by the organized comings and goings of health workers and friends. All these various tasks don't prevent me from sitting in silence beside Inge's bed and watching her, finding myself still hoping for an improvement and the possibility of having a few more years, or even just a few months, before we're separated forever. But I know the verdict is hopeless and the truth is that I'm not able to accept the inexorable progress of the disease. I arrive at the conclusion that my desire to prolong the agony is a selfish and masochistic side of love. Inge's condition creates great suffering for us both, but it is she who has to bear the heaviest physical and emotional suffering. I look at the pain on her face as she sleeps and I recognize behind the mask of the disease the features of my beloved companion. I remember when I used to wake her in the morning with a kiss and she would open her eyes smiling and abandon herself in my arms. In a week's time she will be forty-one years old. I decide to suggest we hold a big party. I pick up the list of friends who have promised me their time and add the names of other people who are dear to us. I try to imagine what a party might be like under these circumstances, and thinking through the various possibilities, I plan how to organize a gathering of thanks and farewell.

Inge wakes. She notices she's home and sees me next to her bed. When our eyes meet, she smiles. I take her hand in mine. We remain in silence for a long time. It is a silence full of all the certainties that have allowed us to face the trials that life has sent us. A silence that gives voice to emotions and memories and so speaks of the love that unites us and the richness of our experience. Inge smiles and cries.

'It's so hard to die. What a lot of energy it takes to do it! But by your side I'll manage, and I'll make it soon. I only want to ask you for one thing: you have to promise me that you'll keep me at home. I don't ever want to go back to the hospital.'

'I promise,' I say, and hold her in my arms to let her know that I'll protect her, and that nothing will shake this resolution.

We remain side by side. I'm aware that the rhythm of Inge's breathing has slowed. I try to breathe in time with her and find that it's impossible for me to maintain the long periods of apnea. This discovery frightens me. Meanwhile Béate arrives. She already has a house key, so, as agreed, she comes in quietly without ringing the bell. She announces her presence by sitting at the piano and playing one of the arias Inge loves. After a quarter of an hour I go out to greet her and ask her to go in to Inge because I need to leave for a couple of hours.

'How is she today?'

'She's happy to be home. We have to get organized so that we can provide her with the same level of comfort and quality of care that she had in hospital. We'll manage, you'll see, and Inge won't find herself regretting her decision to come home. Today's Friday; by Sunday, with help from all of you, I'll need to have everything organized so that, from next week on, all the care will function like clockwork.'

I leave as Béate goes towards Inge's room. She stops at the door because she hears Inge on the phone. Inge has decided to call her mother herself, without waiting for me to give her the latest news gradually and diplomatically. Lisa, Inge's mother, is in Germany. She isn't aware yet that we've come to the end.

'Poor woman, who knows how shocked she'll be to receive this call!', thinks Béate.

'Hello, Mum. I came home from the hospital. I think you should come sooner. Try to leave as soon as possible. I'd like to...'

Inge is distressed and unable to speak. It's too much for her to also have to worry about her mother and deal with the anguish this request will cause and the alarm her mother will feel about Inge's state of health. Béate is uncertain whether she should go into Inge's room and perhaps talk to Lisa on the phone, but Inge begins to speak again: 'I'd like you to be here with us next Thursday for my birthday. You have to make me a *Schokoladenkuchen mit Rhabarber und Sauerrahmeis* [chocolate cake with rhubarb and sour cream ice cream] to remind me of my childhood. Yes ... yes ... no...' says Inge, responding to her mother's questions. 'Call Attilio later if you want to know more. Bye, Mum — see you soon.'

Béate hears that the call is over and goes into the room.

'Hello, Inge. I'm glad to see you're home. I'll come and see you often. Attilio is organizing everything so that you'll have company whenever you want.'

'Yes, there are a number of people I'd like to see here at home. Maybe you'll think it's a bit odd, but I'd like Attilio to organize a birthday party for me next week. Although I won't tell him this, for me it would be like organizing my own funeral with the chance of saying goodbye to the friends I love and whom I'll be sorry to no longer see. I hope he won't be annoyed that I called my mother, but I feel I want to see her one more time.'

The two friends remain in silence for a while, then Inge asks Béate to play again the pieces she used to play herself. The music is still on the piano.

'You play better than me,' Inge tells her, 'I'd like to listen to you; the music calms me. But don't be offended if I fall asleep. If I need you, I'll ring this bell that Attilio has left here on the bedside table. Put it in my hand, please.'

After an hour, Béate goes back to the room. Inge seems to be suffering.

'I feel swollen, as if I'm about to burst. When the nurse comes, I'll have to ask her for something for my stomach.'

Renate, a nurse of about fifty from the palliative care home service, arrives like clockwork at the scheduled time of 6:00 p.m. She says that she's already seen Inge's medical records and has brought her medication with her. She first wants to see what was sent from the hospital and is already available in the house. Her calm and confident manner puts Inge and Béate at ease. Inge says: 'Renate, for some hours now I've been feeling a tightness in my abdomen, as if I were swelling up.'

Renate uncovers and examines her, then straightens the sheet and lightly touches her on her right arm to reassure her.

'We'll hear what the doctor says when he comes. Don't worry. It's a symptom we often see. I'll phone him now to see what time he's planning to visit.'

Half an hour later, I get home at almost the same time as the doctor arrives. Dr Luis Knapen has not met Inge but he's studied her file in the hospital and has spoken to Dr Berditchevsky, the assistant head of the Bordet Institute. Knapen has a competent and reassuring air about him. Before examining Inge he asks her several questions, putting her at her ease and establishing a personal relationship with her. Renate has reported what she's observed. Dr Knapen is concerned but doesn't let it show. He remains a little longer with us then says he'd like to talk to Dr Berditchevsky before treating the swelling that is making Inge suffer.

I accompany him to the door. The doctor tells me, 'It's ascites: an inflammation of the liver has caused an accumulation of fluid in the abdomen. To ease the pain we need to perform a small operation in outpatients; it can't be done at home. We'll have to decide what's best with Dr Berditchevsky.'

'I won't take her back to the hospital,' I say firmly. 'I promised to let her die in peace here at home.'

'It's an unforeseen situation. The swelling is likely to increase during the next twenty-four hours and will make a paracentesis essential, a drainage operation that is usually performed in hospital. Tonight I'll speak to Dr Berditchevsky, then I'll call you.'

I go to my study and phone Guy. I want to understand what exactly the problem is and how it can be resolved without breaking my promise to Inge. Guy explains that, as a rule, a paracentesis is performed in hospital because of the possible complications of bleeding, or the perforation of an intestinal loop. Then he concludes: 'One way or another surgery is necessary and urgent. In the course of two days, up to ten litres of liquid can form and drainage is essential. I want to talk to Knapen and Berditchevsky. We'll take a decision with you.'

Dr Berditchevsky is on night duty at the hospital. At about 9:00 p.m. he calls and tells me to come and see him right away. A family friend is at home and Inge is resting. I leave, promising to be back soon.

In Dr Berditchevsky's office I find the two other doctors: Guy and Knapen. Berditchevsky says that the safest thing would be to bring Inge into the day hospital for a few hours. With the right sedation, she might not even realize she's been moved and, in any case, she would find herself in her room when she woke. In cases such as

Inge's, paracentesis is not practised at home to avoid the risk of serious complications, which can't be totally excluded.

I'd like to cry, but I find an extraordinary strength, and looking Guy in the eyes I say: 'I promised Inge on her deathbed that she'd remain at home until the end. I can't break that promise.'

Guy moves nervously on his chair and says to his colleagues: 'If you help me, I'll take full responsibility and perform the paracentesis at their home.'

I find the strength to say thank you and then go home. Inge is sleeping. I go over to her and whisper, 'We haven't betrayed you.'

The next day is Saturday. At about 9:00 a.m. Guy calls me and says: 'I'll come with Louis de la Roche, a colleague of mine, at about 3 o'clock this afternoon.'

The Mother

Guy, with the help of Dr de la Roche, has performed the paracentesis at home. He has drained five litres of liquid and warns me that it's not to be excluded that more may form in the coming days. The abdominal pain has gradually lessened and everything has taken place without complications. I can really count on Guy. Despite everything, I'm serene because I've had proof that I'll never be alone. I can get on with organizing Inge's birthday party. I need only mention it to three friends from among those who are taking turns to give a hand at home to know there'll be someone to see to the decorations, the music, the drinks, the pizzas, and especially the speeches. Everything will be ready for Thursday.

Now I have to go to the airport to collect Lisa, Inge's mother.

At a standstill in traffic, which is slow and chaotic due to a heavy snowfall, I think of Lisa, a woman of eighty worn out by her hard life. She's going to stay with us, and I'm concerned that living together may prove problematic. The relationship between Inge and Lisa has never been easy, and now, despite her mother's advanced age and her own illness, Inge hopes to make things right with her before she dies. I fear it's an impossible mission.

Lisa is very tired. She wants to rest before she sees Inge. She asks about her illness and repeats that if Inge had gone to Germany for treatment as she'd suggested, she'd probably be on the road to recovery by now. I make no comment and show her to her room.

Now I have another problem to deal with. The new doses of medication prescribed have increased the number of hours that Inge rests, leaving only short periods of lucidity. Under these conditions, even though she eats no more than an occasional spoon of yogurt and drinks almost nothing, Inge, to her great dismay, has become incontinent and needs protection like a baby. This upsets and humiliates her. Fortunately, Rita, a nurse from the hospital, comes to visit her today on her day off.

'Don't worry, Inge, we'll put you at your ease.'

Rita tells me that you can ask the Red Cross to loan a commode free of charge to keep by the bed. We just have to find someone to go and get it. I think of George, one of our stalwart friends. He has a lot of children and therefore a big car that he can use to collect it from the Red Cross depot.

It's Thursday morning when George arrives with his wife, Susanne, to bring the commode, which they've decorated with a big pink bow, as if it were a gift for a young girl. They put it beside the bed, and with George's help I lift the fragile Inge and settle her on the commode. She is semi-conscious. We hear the sound of a few drops falling into the vessel. I give her a kiss on the cheek and say, 'Well done, you've managed!'

We put her back to bed and arrange the pillows.

George hugs Susanne with tears in his eyes and says to her, 'This is the miracle of friendship. A ray of sunlight that's come to warm us in this polar winter. The dignity of a young woman is protected by a commode presented with a pink bow.'

It's 11:00 a.m. Our friends — fifteen in all — have been invited for noon. They arrive one by one, coming in with their own keys, and quietly assemble in Inge's room. Inge has woken from her half-sleep and silently watches her friends who have come to celebrate her birthday. One of them approaches the bed and kneels down in order to be at eye level. He puts the palm of his right hand under Inge's hand, and with his left hand caresses it and then her arm. He says something to her that only she can hear, then rests his head on the bed and Inge begins to stroke his hair back and forth. It's past midday: everyone should have arrived. The pizzas are getting cold in the dining room; the prepared speeches remain in the pockets of those who've written them. In Inge's bedroom there is a silence like the pause between two movements of a symphony.

At a certain point, the doorbell rings. Inge gives a start: 'It's for me. It must be Death. I'm ready. My plan for life and love has been fulfilled. Thank you everyone. Goodbye.'

Inge lies back on the pillows and begins to cry. The tears fall without sobs, as if draining from her heart, which has found through love, solidarity and friendship the meaning of her life.

A shiver runs along the spines of many of the friends gathered around her bed. I move close to Inge while George goes down to open the door. I say to her, 'You're ready, but it's not time yet.'

George, meanwhile, opens the door and welcomes a latecomer. On the ground floor he comes across Lisa, who has come out of her room. George doesn't know her, but easily imagines who this old lady might be.

'I'm a friend of Inge and Attilio's. I imagine you're Inge's mother,' says George, greeting her and showing her to an armchair in the living room. 'Today is Inge's birthday and there are friends in her room who've come to say goodbye.'

Michi, my tabby cat, comes like a flash into the living room. With her fur sleekly groomed, she jumps onto the arm of the chair where Lisa is sitting, as if to say that this is her home. Lisa gives a little start of surprise, then looks closely at her and begins to stroke her head, saying in a trembling voice, 'When Inge was a child she always wanted a cat, but I didn't and so I never let her have one. This cat must have understood and is giving me a lesson. I don't have the courage to go and say hello to Inge. I've made too many mistakes in my life. For weeks I've been tormented, telling myself that I have to go to her. Now I've almost taken that step, but I don't know if I can manage to go and see her. I'll wait until her friends have gone before I go up to her room.'

George has the feeling that Lisa wants to say something else to him, a complete stranger, as if it were a dress rehearsal before going on stage. So he remains silent, waiting.

In Inge's room the atmosphere is hushed and intense. Exhausted by the knowledge of her imminent death and by the painkillers, Inge has fallen into a deep sleep, in a state close to coma. Our friends are moved and speak softly to each other, sharing what they had planned to say during the party, as if their expressions of friendship and love were too intense to remain shut up in their hearts and needed to break out and be communicated. After an hour, they all leave and I remain alone with her.

I walk over to the bed, murmuring tender words of love as I lean over Inge. Her breathing has become even slower. She is far away, submerged in the abyss of coma. Caressing her face I place a kiss on her lips. I feel their slight vibration in return. It is the strongest declaration of love she has ever made me. These moments are precious and will remain in my heart forever.

Lisa has told George many stories about her life and her lack of closeness to Inge. She asks to be left alone for a little while before going up to her daughter's room. George leaves and returns to his work in the city.

In the afternoon, I go down to the living room and find Lisa there, who asks me to accompany her to Inge. We go up to the first floor where Inge is now asleep. Lisa approaches the bed and is shocked to see Inge bald and pallid. Every now and then Inge is shaken by a deep breath and then remains motionless, as if dead. Lisa sits down on a chair at the foot of the bed and watches her, overwhelmed. The cat comes into the room, jumps onto the bed and curls up. Lisa would also like to lie close to Inge and hold her in her arms. She remains in silence on the chair, transfixed. The house is quiet; everything seems to be at a standstill, waiting. At about 6:00 p.m. Dr Knapen arrives and comes into the room. He takes Inge's pulse, measures her blood pressure and sees if new fluid has formed in the peritoneal cavity, all without her waking up. He whispers to me: 'Please cancel all your appointments and stay at home for a few days. Fortunately, a second drainage won't be necessary. It won't be possible to administer certain indispensible drugs orally any more. I'll give the nurses the necessary instructions. An increase in the dose of morphine will produce respiratory depression and accelerate her end. Stay close to Inge. Count on me. I'm more than willing to come back later if I can be of any help. Don't hesitate to call me at any time if you see a change in the situation that requires my attention. Even at the end of her life, Inge has still been able to give you a great gift: the chance to prove to yourself that you are a strong man.'

Lisa is immersed in contemplating her daughter and neither sees nor hears the doctor visiting. She thinks about when Inge was eighteen years old and still living at home with her, her father, and Karin, her sister. It was a fairly normal family and essentially peaceful, at least for the girls, or so it seemed to Lisa, despite financial constraints. When Inge decided to continue her studies in Heidelberg, Lisa had not imagined it would be an almost definitive separation. Although for a number of years they had still shared New Year together, at a certain point it was as if they had grown increasingly distant. Left alone after the death of her husband and Karin's marriage, Lisa had not tried to rebuild her life and had gradually turned in on herself as the infirmities of old age accumulated over the years.

In front of her dying daughter, Lisa realizes she let year after year go by without showing any interest in her, in her studies, her personal life, her work, her marriage or her divorce, and now she finds herself unable to remedy this, or even to communicate her awareness of it to Inge and express her feelings of remorse and love.

While Lisa is deep in her distress, Renate, the home care nurse, arrives. She visits regularly, three times a day, to care for Inge, to see to her dressings and administer the prescribed medicines. Renate has great professional expertise, and her sensitivity and her listening and communication skills are no less great. She has chosen to work in the home care service in order to get away from the frenzied nature of work at the hospital. She earns less now, but her work is rewarding and she does not regret her choice. Renate knows that Lisa is Inge's mother and that she has come a long way. She is immediately aware of the distance that separates her from her daughter. Her experience tells her she can dare, so she tries to engage Lisa in the care she has to give to Inge.

'Excuse me, but I need a hand to make the bed. At the hospital we usually work in pairs. If you help me, we'll disturb Inge as little as possible.'

Renate is very skilful and quick and does not really need Lisa, but she lets her help in order to involve her. She begins to prepare Inge for the night and uncovers her to wash her. Lisa sees the thin body, battered by the mastectomy and laparotomy. Guided by Renate, she finds herself not washing but caressing this suffering body while the tears flow silently down her face. Inge has a nightgown that can easily be changed without disturbing her too much. In the course of making the bed, Renate sees to it that Lisa has to hold Inge's body in her arms. Lisa lingers tenderly on this task while Renate efficiently changes the sheets. Inge slowly comes out of her torpor. She is unable to speak, but signals with a look towards the commode.

Renate whispers to Lisa: 'We have to put her on the commode.'

Lisa holds Inge who relaxes in her arms. Lisa is very moved and remembers when Inge, aged two, was learning to become independent. Now Inge has lost her autonomy, but those who care for her do not offend her dignity. Renate, with an efficient rotating movement, puts Inge back into bed, still involving Inge's mother and giving her the feeling of being indispensable. Inge relaxes in her bed and falls asleep. On her tranquil face, Lisa seems to see the trace of a smile.

Sobbing, Lisa holds Renate and says, 'I've come too late.'

Renate replies, 'I don't think so. People close to death have an awareness and an ability to understand that is totally unexpected. Inge knows that her mother is here, next to her, and that she loves her.'

Lisa remains a long time in the room after Renate leaves, saying she'll return the next morning. It's already dark when I come to join Lisa at Inge's bedside. In the meantime Karin has also arrived.

Inge, watched over by me, her mother and her sister, dies peacefully in the night without regaining consciousness.

Epilogue

People in the terminal phase of an illness are cumbersome, annoying, difficult and useless. Cumbersome with their technological bed, commode, armchair, walking frame, crutches, intravenous drips, catheters and drainage bag: there is no room for them at home. Annoying, with their coughing, wheezing, bad smells, bedsores, insomnia, continuous calls and countless needs. Difficult to manage with their repeated requests, obsessive complaining, and all the other evidence of our impotence. Useless to the economy because they no longer consume; useless to society, in which they have no role to play; and useless to the hospital industry since they do not help the wheels turn. To sum up, people in the final phase of a terminal illness are of no use whatsoever, so let's get it over with as soon as possible . . .

If a request for euthanasia is the result of all this, then it would seem to respond more to the needs of the family, the health service and society than to those of the patient. On the other hand, when a request for euthanasia does come from a patient, in most cases it is prompted by the fear of pain and loneliness, the loss of status in society and the family, or relationships established with caregivers. Yet such a request becomes superfluous and fades when the last phases in life are not dependent on the effectiveness of machines, and when (excluding any futile life-sustaining treatment) physical pain is removed or relieved and the last days are passed in the realm of dignity, personal relationships, friendships and the love that has given life its meaning.[29] In these circumstances, death is no longer a defeat but a challenge to discover the ultimate meaning of life.[30]

Palliative care is the alternative that the new medicine proposes in place of a law that legalizes or decriminalizes euthanasia. It is a medicine that embraces scientific and technological progress, but which has also rediscovered the values and oneness of the individual. Beyond the clinical effectiveness of medical services, this new medicine focuses on caring for patients and sustaining their well-being.

In a world of productivity, efficiency and competitiveness, in a society based on economic activity and superfluous consumption, in which possessions and outward appearance count more than being,[31] there is no room for reflecting on death. In this context, a 'good death' means a quick, painless and unconscious death; if possible, one that disturbs no one, such as dying discreetly in one's sleep.[32]

But if we agree to reject the frenetic activity of modern life,[33] the efficiency of high-tech medicine, and instead propose palliative care; if we admit to our vulnerability and impotence and adopt a serene and accepting attitude,[34] we can help the dying to experience death lucidly, assisting them in a context of relationships, respect, dignity and love in which they accept being loved and giving love, even though the ravages caused by their illness may alter their appearance and cause them distress.

On the basis of my experience in Belgium, which, it should be said, is limited to a single hospital, I have noted that the request for euthanasia is not unusual when patients are admitted in a state of intolerable suffering. Such a request, which in most cases is due to an ideological choice or an incomplete knowledge of the options available, is received respectfully by the medical team, who, how-ever, reserve the right to propose another option in which adequate analgesic measures are adopted, the patients' dignity is guaranteed, and their illnesses are considered in a context of relationships and communication. In the majority of such cases, the initial request for euthanasia is not repeated.

I have become convinced that the right to die in dignity is guar-anteed not so much because the medical act that ends life by means of a lethal injection is not legally punishable under certain condi-tions, but rather by the people and facilities that help patients to live their own death once their physical, psychological and spiritual suffering has been relieved, by allowing them to give meaning to their illness and the time that remains before the end.

To my mind, the act of euthanasia infringes what is generally understood to be the very basis of the doctor's role, especially that of the palliative doctor, who, by accepting to practise euthanasia is implicitly saying to patients that their lives no longer have meaning. Palliative treatment does not have to become the best approach to dealing with the death of terminally sick patients: it remains a form of assistance to people affected by an incurable, mortal disease who deliver themselves up to our care on a journey in which the powers of life intersect with those of death through a search for meaning in the darkness of chaos.[35] In this regard, when Etienne Montero was interviewed by the Commission Sicard,[36] he paraphrased Montesquieu[37] by asserting that 'the absence of law is sometimes more protective of rights'.

The greatest desire of the dying is to have their needs and fears[38] listened to; to be acknowledged as people who have relationships and a role they can still play, and to be respected for their dignity as people, neither compromised nor conditioned by their illness.

People afflicted by a terminal illness teach us to be aware of our weakness, our vulnerability and our impotence. They help us to discover something that subverts our schemes, and they become a resource that aids us in our search for the meaning of life.[39] They offer us — sometimes in spite of themselves — an example and a model: the progressive separation from everything in life that was central to their activities and concerns. They gradually free themselves from all the conditioning that cluttered their existence during the frenzied business of living, and help us to discover that, in the end, all that remains viable and indelible are our experiences and expressions of love.

This includes love we have abandoned or betrayed, or love that ended badly or we are ashamed of, because every sincere expression of love reveals the mysterious universal Love, which is the source of life.[40]

Appendix: Palliative Care and End-of-Life Legislation

Until the nineteenth century in the Western world, caring for the dying and the bereaved was seen primarily as the job of the family and the church. Today, caring for the dying is a new branch of medicine, 'palliative care', which offers specialized care to people suffering from fatal illnesses by maximizing comfort and quality of life when curative treatments are no longer beneficial and the burden of these treatments outweighs their benefits, or when patients are entering the last weeks or months of life. Palliative care is not about dying, but rather about living as well as possible for as long as possible while suffering from a serious illness. The World Health Organisation defines palliative care as follows:

> Palliative care is an approach that improves the quality of life of patients and their families facing the problems associated with life-threatening illness, through the prevention and relief of suffering by means of early identification and impeccable assessment, and treatment of pain and other problems — physical, psychosocial and spiritual.[1]

Palliative care:

- provides relief from pain and other distressing symptoms;
- affirms life and regards dying as a normal process;
- intends neither to hasten nor to postpone death;
- integrates the psychological and spiritual aspects of patient care;
- offers a support system to help patients live as actively as possible until death;
- offers a support system to help the family cope during the patient's illness and in their own bereavement;
- uses a team approach to address the needs of patients and their families, including bereavement counselling, if indicated;
- will enhance quality of life, and may also positively influence the course of illness;
- is applicable early in the course of illness, in conjunction with

other therapies that are intended to prolong life, such as chemotherapy or radiation therapy;

- includes the investigations needed to better understand and
manage distressing clinical complications.

The care offered to the dying is an indicator of how care is provided for all
sick and vulnerable people. It is a measure of society as a whole and a
litmus test for health and social services. In highly developed parts of the
world, palliative care can be regarded as a success. There is evidence of
increasing integration with mainstream health-care provision and the
inclusion of palliative care into national health-care planning processes. In
a few places, specific Palliative Care Strategic Plans have been adopted.[2]
This bodes well, even in times of financial constraint and uncertainty. The
deeper inclusion of palliative care into broader health policy, and the
improvement of standards of end-of-life care, will yield significant gains
for the quality of life. However, countries with a high level of development
in this field of care are very few, and even within these countries there may
be inequity for particular patients, such as those living in peripheral
regions, the very old, those with dementia, or patients who do not fit
comfortably into mainstream society.[3] There is a notable difference
between the rich and poor nations of the world with respect to universal
access to palliative care services. A population of over two billion lives on
less than $1 a day in Africa and India, where government spending on
health is disproportionately low. Out-of-pocket expenses for healthcare
combined with the lack of social security can have a domino effect on poor
families. Despite that, in traditional societies it is rare to find a patient
dying alone in a hospital or nursing home. Family members are actively
involved in providing physical care and companionship. This is an
invaluable resource to build on. However, family involvement has its
negative aspects too. In societies where the family can override the
autonomy of the patient, relatives may demand the continuation of futile
treatments, regardless of the wishes of the patient, or a fatalistic attitude
towards suffering and death may limit care.[4]

The Economist Intelligence Unit (EIU) developed a 'quality of death'
index and recently applied it across 40 countries (30 OECD nations and
10 others for which data was available), measuring numerous indicators

pertaining to the quality of end-of-life care, the cost of end-of-life care, the basic end-of-life healthcare environment, and the availability of end-of-life care. The UK ranked first overall for quality of death, as well as in both the subcategories of availability and quality of end-of-life care.[5] The UK is indeed considered to be both the cradle and pioneer of modern care for the dying. Pain management was first addressed by John Bonica[6] in 1953, but it is Dame Cicely Saunders (1918–2005) who is generally recognized as the founder of the palliative care movement. She trained as a nurse, then as a social worker, and finally as a physician, and was the founder of St Christopher's Hospice in London, which is considered the paradigm for the care of patients at the end of their lives.[7] She studied pain control in terminal illness and introduced the *concept* of 'total pain' (or total suffering, with all its physical, emotional, social and spiritual components), offering a broader approach and framework for the understanding and care of patients at the end of life. Dame Saunders' work has been a source of inspiration and has radiated throughout the world, establishing the hospice and palliative care movement. Experts from the UK, other European countries, Canada and South America have visited St Christopher's to study Dame Saunders' approach, which has been exported and applied to local circumstances.[8]

The compelling reasons for palliative care continue to be better symptom management and improving patients' quality of life. When it comes to financing end-of-life care, governments are not always the only or even the main sources of funding. A range of funding models exists besides public funding, such as church support, philanthropic funds, aid to patients and families having to pay for the services themselves, and, in some cases, hybrid models relying on a mixed range of funding sources. In the UK, a well-established network of non-profit hospices plays an important role in cutting National Health Service expenditure. Charitable funds also support palliative care in Ireland and in other European countries.

However, cost containment is necessary in order to ensure the best use of limited financial resources. Common trends for lowering costs for hospitals, governments and insurance funders include allowing more patients to die at home with better quality care. In every study to date, hospice and palliative care have been associated with equal or better survival and lower costs. This is because savings are generated by a shift away from the use of conventional hospital treatment towards palliative care, by an increase in homecare, and by a reduced use of emergency rooms. [9]

Caring for patients affected by a disease in its terminal phase is raising major ethical questions. Western countries' legislations are converging towards comparable regulations concerning many points, including patients' rights, advanced directives, proxy directives, the refusal of medical treatment, and the duties and responsibilities of medical staff and caregivers. Major differences, however, characterize the evolving legislation on euthanasia or physician-assisted suicide.

In many countries, patients' rights address the following prerogatives of sick people: to receive quality services that respect their dignity and autonomy; to be clearly informed about their state of health; to consult their medical records and obtain a copy or to choose to remain uninformed; to appoint a trusted person to intervene either jointly with them or on their behalf while they are able to exercise their rights, and also a proxy to intervene and represent them if they are not able to exercise their rights; to give their consent to every clinical intervention after having received preliminary information; to express, when in full possession of their mental faculties, their advance healthcare directive, declaring their acceptance or rejection of clinical interventions, including artificial feeding (such statements remaining valid at a later date should patients no longer be capable); and to receive respect with regard to their private life and privacy.

Advanced directives, also called living wills, indicate patients' preferences in terms of treatment options, such as withholding or discontinuing therapy, or refusing artificial feeding. These may also include proxy directives that allow patients to designate a person to represent them when they are no longer able to express their will.

Advanced directives should be easily accessible; for example, embedded in the microprocessor of personal ID-cards. This would make them available in the emergency room should a terminal condition result from an accident. This would assist medical staff in making decisions about patient survival dependent on therapeutic measures with an extreme risk of incurring a persistent vegetative state.

The duties, responsibilities and rights of medical staff and caregivers include a legal guarantee of indemnity from prosecution for health workers; respect for patients' dignity, confidentiality and privacy; respect for patients' right to give their informed consent for refusing or choosing their treatment; to act in the best interests of the patient; to respect in fairness and equality the distribution of scarce health resources and decisions concerning who gets what treatment.

A worldwide hot debate on euthanasia and physician-assisted suicide (PAS) is in course. The WHO considers neither action to be compatible with palliative care and, along these lines, in 2003 the Ethics Task Force of the European Association for Palliative Care (EAPC) produced a paper concluding that the provision of euthanasia and physician-assisted suicide should not be part of the responsibilities of palliative care.[10] In Europe, the European Union leaves policymaking in this area up to the member states. The different approaches in ten countries are addressed in the sections that follow page 137.

Euthanasia is generally defined as an act undertaken 'only by a physician', who intentionally ends the life of a person at the latter's request by administering a lethal substance. To avoid any confusion, in this book I use the term 'euthanasia' in strict accordance with this definition. Some authors call this act *active voluntary euthanasia* and give definitions for non-voluntary euthanasia, involuntary euthanasia and passive euthanasia.[11] Physician-assisted suicide is defined as the self-administration of a lethal substance prescribed by a physician. Euthanasia or physician-assisted suicide are considered criminal offences in most countries. However, euthanasia or PAS — and sometimes both — have been legalized or decriminalised in a small number of countries and states.

To date, the Netherlands has legalized euthanasia (2002), while Belgium (2002) and Luxembourg (2008) have decriminalized it.[12] The laws in the Netherlands and Luxembourg also allow PAS. In the United States, the states of Oregon, Washington, Vermont, New Mexico and Montana legalized PAS between 1997 and 2013, and California might soon be added to the list, following a vote of 11 September 2015 at the State Assembly which would allow terminally ill patients to legally end their lives with PAS if the California Governor will promulgate the Bill.[13] Euthanasia remains illegal in all US states.[14] Switzerland legalized PAS with a referendum in 2011, which approved an interpretation of a law of

1942 that punished assistance in suicide only in the case of non-altruistic motives. Colombia legalized euthanasia in 2010. In the province of Quebec, Canada a new law decriminalizing euthanasia might come into force on 10 December 2015, unless the federal government challenges it.[15] In Australia's Northern Territory euthanasia and physician-assisted suicide were legalized in July 1966, but the Act was in force during only nine months, being voided by the federal Euthanasia Laws Act in 1997.[16] In Switzerland, private, for-profit organizations attract healthy foreigners to cross borders with a view to ending their lives. The German language has introduced a neologism, *Sterbetourismus* [death tourism], to describe this phenomenon. To date, no such practice is reported for euthanasia in the countries that legalized or decriminalized it,[17] although the text of the laws in those countries does not explicitly exclude the request for euthanasia by non-residents.

In all jurisdictions where euthanasia or PAS are regulated by law, safeguards, criteria and procedures have been put in place to control the practices, to ensure societal oversight, and to prevent euthanasia and PAS from being abused or misused. Some criteria and procedures are common across the jurisdictions; others vary from country to country. Prevention measures have included explicit, reiterated consent by the person requesting euthanasia, mandatory reporting of all cases, administration only by physicians (with the exception of Switzerland) and consultation by a second physician.

There is evidence that these safeguards are regularly ignored and transgressed in all the jurisdictions, and that transgressions are not prosecuted. Increased tolerance of transgressions in societies with such laws represents a social 'slippery slope', as do changes in the laws, criteria and practices that have followed legalisation. Although the initial intent was to limit euthanasia and assisted suicide to a last-resort option for a very small number of terminally ill people, some jurisdictions now extend the practice to newborn infants, children, prisoners, psychotic patients and people with dementia. A terminal illness is no longer a prerequisite.[18]

An example of a slippery slope is the misinterpretation of the conditions justifying a 'double effect' (the permissibility of an action that causes a serious harm as a side effect of promoting some good end), which may occur in emergency rooms, or at the scene of murders or road accidents, when accident- or emergency-physicians disguise the mercy killing of agonized individuals as deep sedation.

In this Appendix we will cover the provision of palliative care services and the current status of end-of-life legislation in ten countries, seven of which are English-speaking (Australia [AU], Canada [CA], Ireland [IE], New Zealand [NZ], South Africa [ZA], United States of America [US], United Kingdom [UK]). The remaining three included are European countries, namely Italy (IT), Belgium (BE) and France (FR), with which the author is personally familiar. He has an interest in analyzing the provision of palliative care in Belgium, a country where euthanasia is decriminalized, and in France, where the debate on end-of-life legislation has raised an ethical question of general relevance, and where a step forward in legislation was attempted and failed in 2015. Seven out of the ten countries covered in this appendix were among the ten top countries according to EIU's above-mentioned Quality of Death index (in order: UK, AU, NZ, IR, BE, CA, US).[19]

Italy

The first palliative care unit in Italy was created in 1980 at the National Cancer Institute of Milan, where in 1988 the European Association for Palliative Care was founded, with Vittorio Ventafridda as its first President.

Legal aspects

Now, more than thirty-five years later, palliative care is regulated by law no. 38/2010: Provisions to ensure access to palliative care and pain therapy.[20] This law defines palliative care as a combination of therapeutic and diagnostic measures and assistance. These measures concern patients and their families and focus on the active and complete care of individuals suffering from a disease whose progression compromises their survival and does not respond to curative therapies. This law recognizes patients' right of access to palliative care and pain therapy and protects their dignity and the quality of life until death. It guarantees appropriate support for patients and their families, ensures the presence of adequate healthcare facilities, promotes awareness campaigns and the training of healthcare personnel, and guarantees adequate funding.

Law no. 38/2010 does not address euthanasia or PAS. Any act where the doctor's primary intention is to bring about a patient's death is unlawful in Italy. The law does not cover advance healthcare directives. Advance healthcare directives have been the subject of several bills that were never approved due to the strong resistance that bioethical arguments encounter in the Italian political world as a result of ideological pressure, manipulation and populist support from the more conservative positions of Catholic culture.

Aside from my strong reservations about the absence of provisions for advance healthcare directives, the law is well structured and takes advantage of the experience of countries that legislated on these matters several years earlier. However, its conversion into regional legislation and decrees on its implementation are still not operational in some regional jurisdictions. Similarly, neither the culture of palliative care nor its practice is evenly spread throughout the country.

Where palliative care is provided

The Italian public health service guarantees palliative care in designated hospital wards of renowned excellence in a number of large hospitals, but especially in 231 hospices with a total of 2,551 beds, each with between ten and thirty beds. These are specialized, autonomous centres that receive patients at the terminal stage and also provide adequate support for their families.[21] The model is inspired by England's St Christopher's Hospice, a centre with seventy beds in the southeast suburbs of London, founded by Dame Cicely Saunders in 1967. Law no. 39/1999 (Provisions to ensure the urgent implementation of the national health plan)[22] allocated considerable funds to the regions for the development of hospices, and thereby radically changed the scenario for palliative care in Italy.

In addition, Italy also has an efficient palliative care home service, involving doctors, nurses, psychologists, social workers and trained volunteers, who are coordinated at a provincial level in a network that ensures specialized assistance, ranging from palliative care doctors to family general practitioners (GPs). In some provinces, each hospice ensures health coverage for a number of home beds equal to three times the number of hospice beds. In other provinces, the assistance and advice service for GPs is provided by a provincial organization that sees to the coordination of medical care and home nursing, even in rural areas far from centres with a hospice.

In Italy there are 3.9 hospice beds for palliative care for every l00,000 residents. The Ministry of Health believes that the optimal number should be 6.0. Home care compensates the gap: the waiting time for hospice acceptance has been a maximum of three days in 70 per cent of cases in 2014.[23]

Information on palliative care and the available resources can be found on the website of the Italian Ministry of Health[24] and on the site of the Italian Society for Palliative Care (SICP).[25] The latter describes the structure of SICP (headed by a president and a national council elected by members for a three-year term), its activities, its mission and its organization at the local level. It also provides information on the regional offices where citizens can find a response to their request for assistance for their loved ones.

Cost of palliative care

In Italy, citizens contribute to national public health spending through general taxation in proportion to their income and, if not entitled to an exemption, through the payment of a specific ticket for the provision of some services, among which palliative care is not included. Palliative care in hospitals, hospices, or in other settings is covered by public funding.

Belgium

Belgium is a democratic, multicultural country torn by geographic, linguistic, economic and ideological divisions. Its Christian base has conservative, traditionalist roots and maintains control of most schools, universities and hospitals, in opposition to a secular, atheist and, in part, masonic component. These two cultures coexist tolerantly as a result of systematic compromises and without the confessional constraints that powers outside state institutions impose in other countries. When a coalition presents a non-negotiable request it can be adopted, while at the same time guaranteeing the implementation of compensatory measures proposed by the opposite faction. Although this practice provides an exit from situations of political impasse, it may at times aggravate existing rifts.

Legal aspects

To complement a law decriminalizing euthanasia, the cultural and political plurality of parliamentary representation adopted two other ideologically opposed laws regarding the rights of the sick and palliative care. In 2002, after long years of Christian Democratic rule, a favourable political environment brought about by a new, rainbow-coalition government enabled topics to be addressed that had once been taboo: prostitution, drugs, homosexuality and the end of life. Within four months, Belgium adopted three laws pertaining to patients' rights and the end of life: the law of 28 May 2002 on euthanasia,[26] the law of 14 June 2002 on palliative care,[27] and the law of 22 August 2002 concerning patients' rights.[28]

The primary purpose of the palliative care law is to provide relief from pain for patients affected by an illness at a terminal stage, while assuring them and their loved ones maximum autonomy and the best possible quality of life. A multidisciplinary team ensures assistance to dying patients, with particular regard to the physical, mental, social and moral aspects of their situation. The law also provides for improving the provision of palliative care and ensuring the training of staff and GPs.

The law on patients' rights covers advance directives, the right to privacy, the right to access one's medical record, to appoint a trusted person and a proxy, and the right to refuse treatment, including artificial feeding.

The euthanasia law has decriminalized the act of euthanasia without legalizing it – in other words, the Penal Code was not amended (in contrast with legislation in the Netherlands). Euthanasia therefore remains premeditated murder with the vulnerability of the victim a possible aggravating factor, but the doctor who carries out this act under the conditions and according to the procedures prescribed by law cannot be prosecuted. The law does not confer a right to euthanasia but an entitlement to request it. It allows doctors access to it without exposing them to criminal proceedings and without them being required to give an affirmative response to the request. The act of euthanasia can only be practised by a doctor (after consultation with a second, independent doctor) if the request is expressed and reaffirmed by an adult patient affected by an incurable disease that is causing intolerable suffering. Patients must be free to choose, and physicians must inform them about the possibilities offered by palliative care. The law on euthanasia states that individuals can make a request for euthanasia in their advance healthcare directive, provided that certain conditions are met. Legally, death by euthanasia is incorporated under natural death, also with regard to related fiscal, inheritance and insurance matters.

The euthanasia law was amended in 2014 by a further law that extended decriminalization to euthanasia practised on minors. The law does not stipulate an age limit.[29] Minors must be gravely ill and enduring suffering that cannot be relieved and will lead to death in the short term. The request must be made on a voluntary basis, reflected upon several times, and must not derive from external pressure. Minors must be certified to be of sound mind and sentient at the time of the request. Parental consent is also required.

Out of a population of about 11 million inhabitants, 104,000 deaths are reported in Belgium each year, of which 31,000 are due to cancer or degenerative diseases. The number of deaths by euthanasia has increased in recent years, passing from 235 cases in 2003 to 1,816 cases in 2013. In the majority of these cases (51 per cent), euthanasia is practised at home or in care homes. It is estimated that the number of unreported deaths by euthanasia is comparable to the number officially recorded, and that this number has not seen a decrease since the adoption of the law.

The application of the law governing euthanasia is *a posteriori* [after the fact] and monitored by a federal commission to which the doctor who practised euthanasia must provide a detailed report within four days of the patient's death. There are no sanctions for the doctor who does not provide such a report, nor a check on the conditions under which the act took place. Verification after the fact cannot be considered sufficient for protecting patients from practices carried out in violation of the law.

The commission analyses the reports, and, in the case of irregularities, may decide by a two-thirds majority to submit a file to the public prosecutor within two months of the patient's death. Every two years the commission makes a report to Parliament, which includes statistics, assessments and recommendations. The law stipulates that the composition of the commission should be balanced ideologically, linguistically and in terms of gender, yet most members belong to pro-euthanasia associations, and the rule that a two-thirds majority is required to submit a dossier to the judiciary prevents the consideration of minority opinions. Witness the fact that during the thirteen years since the adoption of the law, no file has ever been submitted to the public prosecutor. In essence, the commission conducts statistical analyses on cases that doctors who practise euthanasia have decided they want to present.[30]

On the other hand, cases of physician-assisted suicide have been documented. So have applications of the law that go beyond the intention of the legislation expressed in 2002, including the illegal practice of delegating the act of euthanasia to nurses.

A survey from 2008 mentioned by Etienne Montero indicates that the number of cases of clandestine euthanasia, more than 1,000 a year according to estimates, has not declined since the adoption of the law.[31]

The 2014 extension of the law was passed by an overwhelming majority (89/44). A number of surveys show that the population is in favour of euthanasia and the extension of its application. An article published in a specialist magazine[32] announced the end of the conflict between euthanasia and palliative care (although with such strong optimism that it conjures doubt), and the absence of any dangerous leanings towards further extensions of the law.[33]

In contrast, in the *European Journal of Palliative Care*, a team from the Flanders Federation of Palliative Care published a study that describes how palliative care professionals in Flanders give daily assistance to citizens asking for euthanasia; a decade after the introduction of the decriminalization law of 2002, the same team claimed that, since the law had been passed, euthanasia had developed its own dynamic and had gone beyond the legal restrictions, contrary to explicit declarations issued beforehand that guaranteed there would be no extension.[34]

With regard to the law's extension to children, many authoritative Belgian paediatricians had asked in vain for further and deeper reflection before the final parliament debate, citing several arguments:

- the absence of a request for euthanasia in their clinical practice;
- the existence of adequate means to relieve suffering;
- the complexity of assisting paediatric patients suffering from serious disease, and the risk of children being affected by pressure from their parents, or by their suffering, and thus feeling they must end their lives;
- the difficulty of assessing with certainty if a minor has sufficient mental capacity to make an informed decision.

The 2014 extension of the 2002 law was apparently ideologically motivated and conditioned by the competitive climate of an upcoming general election. It opened the way to dangerous extensions of the law to include patients who are unable make a request, such as infants or the insane, individuals suffering from degenerative diseases, psychotic patients, prisoners, not to mention euthanasia justified on economic grounds. It also evokes an association between euthanasia and the explantation of organs for future transplants, which certain hospitals already practise in adjacent operating theatres.[35]

A doctor who styled herself as Catholic published a book to explain why and how she practises euthanasia in Belgium, and describes how euthanasia is being ritualized in her hospital with the participation of the caregivers' team, which includes a Catholic priest.[36]

Euthanasia risks being trivialized, it risks establishing itself as an ethically acceptable act and becoming a therapeutic resource for doctors to use when dealing with the suffering of dying patients, or even being considered as a palliative care option once the prohibition on killing is removed and every reference to values is lost.

Where palliative care is provided

Thirteen years after the adoption of the three laws outlined above, palliative care units now exist in hospitals in every province. In-patient palliative care is complemented by a nationwide network of home care for patients affected by illness in a terminal phase. Both hospital-based and home-based services are coordinated by effective, interconnected territorial organizations integrated into three regional entities. They guarantee the diffusion of palliative care, the permanent training of healthcare personnel and volunteers, and the immediate availability of resources to assist the terminally ill. In Belgium, there are 6.8 palliative care hospital beds available for every 100,000 residents. The Ministry of Health considers that 9.0 would be necessary.

This situation offers a choice of two possibilities: to be assisted to a natural end of life relying on palliative care, or the free and regulated choice of an act that puts an end to life.

In comparison with other hospital wards, palliative care units are equipped with more resources since they do not have to satisfy the same criteria of financial viability; moreover, the number of healthcare personnel available is three times above the average of other wards. These conditions enable the adequate control of each symptom, and, in 90 per cent of cases, pain is reduced. Patients can spend their last days in a peaceful environment where there is space for the relationships and emotional ties that have given meaning to their lives.

Cost of palliative care

The law relating to palliative care provides that each patient should be able to benefit from palliative care within the framework of end-of-life assistance. Entities that contribute palliative care, and the criteria for reimbursement of such treatment by the social security system, must guarantee equal access to palliative care for all incurable patients as part of the provision of overall healthcare. As a result of the consolidation and financing of entities that provide palliative care in hospitals and at home, the nationwide waiting time for admittance to palliative care services is only a few days.

Family members of patients admitted to palliative care units are entitled to paid leave and other forms of assistance and financial support, according to the provisions and regulations ordained by law.

France

The implementation of palliative care in hospitals, socio-medical institutions, or even at home, is meant to provide a solution for patients who wish to end their days in an environment that above all alleviates their psychological and physical suffering and offers them a peaceful atmosphere. And yet at the core of French society there is a daily increase in support of the legitimization of euthanasia from the great majority of people (80–90 per cent according to opinion polls). This is despite all the reservations expressed by many of these same individuals regarding the risks related to the legalisation of euthanasia and, primarily, the risk of abusing such a right. It seems that in French society there has been a shift in the concept of the value of human life. A noticeable transformation in social conventions is underway, whereby a life is considered to have value only when it is 'useful'; in other words, when a person is able to act, produce, or be considered cost-effective. A 'good death' is affirmed as the ultimate expression of freedom. The same applies to the time it takes to die. People can no longer bear the wait. It is deemed unnecessary, distressing for the family, and considered by some as a waste of time – time that could be better spent on more useful activities. The utilitarian value at times given to life promotes the idea that its end has no meaning. And if it is meaningless, then we should be able to terminate it. Hence the idea of a rapid death is viewed favourably, and assisting a dying person loses its meaning for society.

Legal aspects

French legislation dealing with the end of life is based on the Léonetti law, no. 2005-370 (2005), concerning patients' rights and the end of life.[37] It was preceded by law no. 99-477 (1999), which aimed to guarantee the right of access to palliative care,[38] and law no. 2002-303 (2002) regarding the rights of the sick and the quality of the health service.[39]

Law no. 2005-370 pursues three objectives: to relieve the anxieties of those who legitimately fear the end of life, to allay the fears of health professionals who desire legal guarantees, and to reconcile patients' rights to freely decide on treatment with health workers' needs for legal indemnity.[40] It aims to establish the primacy of the quality of life over and above its duration and states that all adults may draw up an advance healthcare directive for a future time when they may no longer be able to express their will. It also allows patients to require doctors to withhold, reduce, withdraw, or not initiate treatment deemed ineffective, disproportionate or futile when the sole purpose is the artificial prolongation of life. The law also authorizes sedation in the terminal phase of an illness, administered in order to relieve patients from what is considered to be unbearable suffering, regardless of the consequences this sedation may cause.

During the campaign for the presidential election in 2012, François Hollande committed to 'evolving legislation on end-of-life and accompaniment to death'. Once elected, the President assigned to Didier Sicard, former president of the National Consultative Ethics Committee, the task of assessing law 2005-370, as part of a reflection on the end of life. The Sicard Committee report entitled *Penser solidairement la fin de vie* [Thinking Integrally about the End of Life] was presented on 18 December 2012. It is an in-depth account of the end-of-life situation in France, extracts of which are reproduced in these pages.[41]

In its conclusions, the Sicard Report calls for significant effort to be made to encourage society, together with doctors and health workers, to fully adhere to the Léonetti law. Moreover, it proposes that the effectiveness of earlier legislation should be ensured (the 1999 law relating to access to palliative care; the law of 2002 on patients' rights, and the Léonetti law itself of 2005), and that new laws regarding the end-of-life in emergency situations should not be adopted. The report suggests a series of measures to be taken by the relevant public authorities, these include:

- campaigns regarding the importance of preparing advance directives;
- university courses on palliative care;
- consolidating training programmes on neonatology and encouraging reflection on futile medical treatment;
- introducing palliative care from the first day a serious disease is diagnosed;

- avoiding the unreasonable prolongation of life in emergency departments;
- giving visibility on the internet to the different sources and expertise available;
- widening the possibility of paid leave from work for family members of terminally ill patients;
- performing – after a collegial discussion – deep sedation in the last stages of end-of-life care when patients in a terminal condition expressly request the interruption of all treatment that could prolong life, including nutrition and hydration, or have in their medical record an official advance healthcare directive that contains such a request.

The publication of the Sicard Report initiated a spirited debate in French society and in the French Parliament. On 17 March 2015, a legislative proposal on the end-of-life amending the 2005 Léonetti law was adopted in the National Assembly by 436 to 34 votes with 83 abstentions.[42] However, on 17 June, when this new legislative proposal approved by the lower chamber was read before the senate, after a lively and passionate debate it was ultimately defeated with a vote of 87 to 196.[43] The legislative proposal did not authorize euthanasia or assisted suicide, but it established new rights in favour of the sick and the terminally ill, marking a very important step forward. Rather than favouring the doctor's point of view, the proposal supports that of the patient. It would have enforced absolute respect for advance directives, allowing caregivers to implement patients' instructions as specified in their will. It would have enforced the right to 'profound and continuing' sedation until death for terminally ill patients, including withholding all life-sustaining treatments that aim to artificially prolong the life of patients who do not wish to endure an incurable disease. And it would have provided for the continuation, development and improved provision of palliative care.

The palliative care situation

The French Society of Palliative Care provides an overview of the history of palliative care on its website.[44] The first palliative care treatment dispensed to the terminally ill took place in Lyon in 1842, but it was not until the 1980s, in the wake of the examples set by Britain and Quebec, Canada, that palliative care developed in France.

At the present time, palliative care units in hospitals and networks of home-based palliative care provided by mobile teams have a good reputation, and the doctors, health workers and volunteers working in this area are, in general, highly respected by the public. Each of the previously illustrated solutions receives specific funding.

According to a 2008 estimate mentioned in the Sicard Report, there were at that time 322,000 individuals per year requesting the provision of palliative care out of 535,000 deaths among people older than nineteen years of age. The provision of such care has been constantly growing since 2007 and currently amounts to 1,314 beds in palliative care units plus a further 5,057 designated hospital beds, although the latter are not all used solely for this purpose. One thousand beds can accommodate 20,000 dying patients per year, thus the resources available serve 126,000 patients, or 40 per cent of the demand. Bearing in mind the number of patients receiving treatment at home, the provision is close to satisfying total requirements. France, however, has wide geographical disparities in providing palliative care, especially in the provinces, where all too often patients die in unacceptable conditions in accident and emergency departments.

Cost of palliative care

Palliative care is accessible to everyone, at any age, and is covered by health insurance at home, in hospitals, clinics, socio-medical institutions for the handicapped and mentally ill, and nursing homes, where there are 'allocated beds' and specialist palliative care health workers.[45]

United Kingdom

The United Kingdom pioneered palliative care and continues to be the European leader in its development in terms of the quantity of services offered, the high standards expected and the research undertaken. The UK ranked first overall in the 2010 Economist Intelligence Unit's quality of death survey[46] for quality of death, as well as in both the subcategories of availability and quality of end-of-life care. The UK is currently developing a full End of Life Care Strategy – the first of its kind in the world.[47] However, Britain suffers a shortage of medical personnel working in palliative care, and many vacant posts remain unfilled due to an insufficient number of qualified applicants. Training is also an issue, as is the availability of medication outside normal working hours. These challenges are likely to increase in future years because the demand for palliative care in the UK, as in any other country, is expected to rise as a consequence of an ageing population.

Around 600,000 people die in the UK each year, half a million of these in England, out of whom about 350,000 need palliative care.[48] Of this group, 170,000 receive specialist palliative care and 80,000 have their needs met by other general services. Most deaths occurring in this early part of the twenty-first century follow a period of chronic illness, such as heart disease, cancer, stroke, chronic respiratory disease, neurological disease or dementia. Most deaths (58 per cent) occur in National Health Service (NHS) hospitals, around 18 per cent occur at home, 17 per cent in care homes, 4 per cent in hospices and 3 per cent elsewhere.[49] An independent review prepared for the Secretary of State for Health (2011) reported that in the UK about 20 per cent of the people in need of proper palliative care are not being reached.[50]

In the United Kingdom during the 1980s,[51] three factors conjoined to build a framework for the broad consolidation of the new field of palliative care: a medical association was formed to support its practitioners,[52] a scientific journal was established,[53] and the UK became the first country in the world to recognize palliative medicine as an area of specialization.

In 1987, palliative medicine was established as a sub-specialization of general medicine, initially on a seven-year trial period, which, when successfully concluded, led to the creation of the specialization in its own right, supported today by a number of academic centres, professorial chairs and dedicated institutes.[54] The four-year training programme in the United Kingdom was designed to equip trainees with skills to practise palliative medicine in any setting. Importantly, United Kingdom programmes also require competence in a range of essential management skills, including recruiting and managing staff, and service development.

Patients' rights

In 2012, the UK government issued the NHS Constitution.[55] Everyone who is cared for by the NHS in England has legal rights that cover access to health services, quality of care and environment, treatments and drugs, consent and confidentiality, patient choice of treatment, receipt of healthcare based on medical need and no other factor, registration with a general practitioner (GP), the right to change GP without difficulty, the right to emergency treatment, the right to a second opinion under certain circumstances, the right to give informed consent for treatment, the right of access to health records and an assurance of their confidentiality, the right to decline to participate in medical research and medical training, and the right to complain and receive compensation.

Legal aspects

The legal aspects of end-of-life care continue to evolve in the UK as they do in many other countries. At the time of writing, euthanasia is illegal throughout the UK, and any act where the doctor's primary intention is to bring about a patient's death is unlawful.[56] However, as a matter that has been devolved to the Scottish Parliament, it is possible that at some point in the future, different laws on euthanasia could apply within the UK. A bill aiming to give terminally ill patients the right to die at their request did not pass through Parliament before the May 2015 general election. The Assisted Dying Bill, under discussion in Parliament in early 2015, would have provided assistance for 'competent' adults with a life expectancy of less than six months to end their lives at their own request.[57,58] A new unsuccessful attempt to pass legislation on the matter in the current period of office of the House of Commons resulted in the submission of the same Bill with some changes later in 2015. The House of Commons rejected the Assisted Dying bill by 330 votes to 118, a majority of 212, after an emotional debate on 11 September 2015.[59]

In England and Wales, people may make an advance directive or appoint a proxy under the Mental Capacity Act 2005. This only pertains to a future refusal of treatment if the patient lacks mental capacity, and has to be considered valid and applicable by the medical staff concerned.[60] People are often encouraged to prepare both documents in order to provide comprehensive guidance regarding their care.

Doctors have a duty in law to protect the life and foster the health of patients. A number of legal judgements on withholding and withdrawing treatment have shown that the courts do not consider that the protection of life always takes precedence over other considerations. Case law establishes a number of relevant principles. Capable adult patients may decide to refuse treatment even if refusal may result in harm to themselves or in their own death. Life prolonging treatment can lawfully be withheld or withdrawn from patients who lack capacity, if starting or continuing such treatment is not in their best interests. There is no obligation to give treatment that is futile or burdensome. If adult patients have lost their capacity, a refusal of treatment made when they were capable must be respected, provided it is clearly applicable to the present circumstances and there is no reason to believe that they changed their mind.

Where palliative care is provided

The demographics of death in relation to age, cause of death and place of death have changed radically over the course of the past century. In the early years of the twentieth century, most people died in their own homes. However, over the course of the last century, familiarity with death within society as a whole has decreased. Many people nowadays do not experience the death of someone close to them until they are well into midlife. In Britain, as in many other countries, people do not discuss death and dying openly.

Although every individual may have a different idea about what, for them, would constitute a 'good death', for many this would involve being treated as an individual with dignity and respect, being without pain and other symptoms, being in familiar surroundings, and being in the company of close family and/or friends.

Some people do indeed die as they would have wished, experiencing excellent care in hospitals, hospices, care homes and in their own homes. But the reality is that many do not. Many people experience unnecessary pain and other symptoms. There are distressing reports of people not being treated with dignity and respect, and many people do not die where they would choose. Access to good services is inconsistent, and the absence of sufficient provision for 24/7 community services is notable. Research consistently shows that most people in the UK (between 56 per cent and 65 per cent of adults) would like to be cared for and die in their own home, but the great majority (58 per cent) still die in hospital, and arguably at a higher economic cost.

In the past, end-of-life care within the NHS and care services had a relatively low profile. Reflecting this, the quality of care delivered has been very variable and there are significant challenges to address. Palliative care in England is provided by a plurality of providers from both the NHS and the voluntary sector. Unfortunately, there is a lack of integration and coordination among services and the provision of palliative care varies among geographical areas.

Implementation of the End of Life Care Strategy promises to be a step forward in improving access to high quality care for everyone in the UK approaching the end of life. This should be irrespective of age, gender, ethnicity, religious belief, disability, sexual orientation, diagnosis or socio-economic status. High quality care should be available wherever the patient may be, at home or elsewhere.

The NHS palliative care team will organize patients to be cared for according to their wishes once a full care assessment has identified exactly what the care requirements are. NHS assistance can often commence within 48 hours of a patient's initial enquiry.

Patients may not need to move away from home to receive care since hospice care can also be provided at home and is sometimes available as a 24-hour service. In practice, care can be provided at home, in a hospital, in a hospice, or in a care home. In hospitals there are specialist palliative care teams who work alongside and support the hospital doctors, nurses and other health and social care professionals. If they so wish, patients can also receive end-of-life care in a care home, where trained staff are available to look after them at all times. People choosing to receive care at home, in a care home or in a hospice are advised to check with their GP or consult the NHS continuing healthcare service.[61]

Financial aspects

The National Health Service in the United Kingdom operates under central management from the Department of Health and is funded through general taxation. Healthcare services are free of user fees at the point of access. Various staff members working in NHS health and social care and the independent sector can provide palliative care across all care settings. A combination of NHS resources and the voluntary sector funds palliative care; as a consequence, there is no payment required for palliative care consultation, hospitalization or medications.[62] If someone such as a partner or relative is looking after a patient, they may be eligible, as a carer, for local authority help, such as respite care.

Hospice costs are covered in the UK by the Department of Health and by donations from the community. A recent survey by the Department of Health[63] estimates that primary care trusts (administrative bodies responsible for commissioning health services) spent £460m on adult palliative and end-of-life care in 2010/11. A large number of hospice services in England are managed and predominantly funded by the voluntary sector, operated either as independent hospices or by national specialist charities. The funding that voluntary sector organizations receive from the state does not normally cover their full running costs. On average, adult hospices in England received 34 per cent of their running costs from government funds. The actual percentage of state funding for local charitable hospices around the country varies considerably – from zero to 62 per cent of their costs.

Both NHS and independent hospices providing care to adults or children can apply for grants to enhance the hospice environment.[64] In addition, considerable other funds are made available to hospice and palliative care providers each year. These come from a number of sources, including the communities they serve. Other organizations, such as national associations like Help the Hospices or grant-making entities, make funds available for palliative care.

United States of America

In the American healthcare system there is no single government provider since the organization consists of several tiers set within a federal system of government.[65] Government healthcare roles are at federal, state and local level. In the United States, hospice programmes began in the 1970s, and Medicare funding was secured in 1982 (providing reimbursement of costs through insurance, but requiring relinquishment of curative treatments).[66]

Palliative care services and hospice care

Today, palliative care is a central part of treatment for serious or life-threatening illnesses.[67] Ideally, palliative care should be initiated concurrently with a diagnosis of a serious illness and at the same time as curative or disease-modifying treatments, given the near universal occurrence of patient and family distress and their need for information and support in establishing achievable goals for the patient's medical care. The National Institute of Health (NIH) informs citizens to help them understand how patients or someone close to them can benefit from this type of care. The NIH defines palliative care as the comprehensive treatment of the discomfort, symptoms and stress of a serious illness. Palliative care does not replace the patient's primary treatment and works together with it, providing relief from distressing symptoms, among them pain, shortness of breath, fatigue, constipation, nausea, loss of appetite and problems with sleep. It can also help patients deal with the side effects of the medical treatments they are receiving. Perhaps most importantly, palliative care can help improve the quality of life for patients and their families alike.

Palliative care is different from hospice care, which focuses on a person's final months of life. Contrary to the meaning of hospice care in Europe (where it is intended as patient care in a particular setting, namely the hospice), hospice care in the US is a model of quality, compassionate care for people facing a life-limiting illness that is offered in the patient's home, but may also be provided in independent hospice centres, hospitals, nursing homes, or other long-term care facilities.[68]

Palliative care also provides support for a patient's family and can improve communication between patients and their healthcare providers, as well as offering emotional and spiritual support for both. Palliative care is provided by a team of specialists who may include palliative care doctors, palliative care nurses, trained volunteers, social workers, chaplains, pharmacists, nutritionists, counsellors and others. The Palliative Care Provider Directory of Hospitals helps in searching for a hospital that offers a palliative care programme in any US state and city.[69]

Hospice services are available to patients with any terminal illness, regardless of age, religion or race. Members of the hospice staff make regular visits to assess the patient and to provide additional care or other services. Hospice staff are on call twenty-four hours a day, seven days a week. The hospice team develops a care plan that meets each patient's individual needs for pain management and symptom control. The National Hospice and Palliative Care Organization (NHPCO) estimates that in 2012, 400,000 hospice volunteers provided 19 million hours of service, spending time with patients and families, providing clerical and other services, and helping with fundraising efforts.

In 2013, the number of deaths in the US was 2.6 million out of a population of 321 million. The percentage of US deaths served by hospice care is 61 per cent and steadily increasing over the years.[70] In 2011, the average length of hospice care was 18.7 days, and a few patients received more than 180 days of care. Until recently, palliative care services were typically available only to patients enrolled in hospice centres. Now, however, in addition to other settings, palliative care programmes are found increasingly in hospitals, which are a main location for the care of the seriously ill and, on average, the place of death for 50 per cent of adults nationwide. In 2009, 62 per cent of US hospitals with at least 50 beds and 84 per cent of hospitals with more than 300 beds reported having a palliative care programme, which is an increase of 134 per cent since 2000.[71]

Where palliative care is provided

The majority (96.5 per cent) of patient care is provided in the place the patient calls 'home'. In addition to private residences, this includes nursing homes and residential facilities. In 2012, 66 per cent of patients received care at home. The percentage of hospice patients receiving care in a hospice inpatient facility was 27 per cent.

Hospice services in the US developed from the New Haven, CT organization, founded in 1974, to some 3,000 US hospices at the turn of the century.[72] Dame Cicely Sanders, the founder of St Christopher's Hospice in London, lectured from coast to coast in the US on pain management and total care for the dying from 1963 onwards, and doctor Elisabeth Kübler-Ross had been running seminars on the dying at the Billings Hospital in Chicago, IL, since 1969. In the US today, the focus on home care and the idea of hospital teams and inpatient hospice beds is less developed than in other Western countries. A major milestone in 1982 was the achievement of funding recognition for hospices under the US Medicare programme.

Access to palliative care and hospice programmes is widely variable across the country. For-profit hospitals, hospitals in the southern US, and small, safety net hospitals (fewer than 100 beds) are less likely to report hospital palliative care programmes compared to not-for-profit hospitals, hospitals outside the South, and larger hospitals. Access to hospice care is also highly variable. Based on 2006 data, it covered as low as 6.7 per cent of all deaths in Alaska, to as high as 44.7 per cent of deaths in Arizona.[73]

Legal aspects

In 1973, some twenty years prior to the publication of the Patient's Charter in England,[74] the American Hospital Association published the Patient Bill of Rights, the first document in America to express the rights of patients while in hospital.[75] The Patient Bill of Rights was used to express what all patients should expect in hospital, while at the same time providing a tangible means by which hospitals could express their commitment to their patients. The document had a strong influence on hospitals throughout America and ultimately influenced many states to develop their own distinctive patient rights bills. One of the best examples is the State of New Jersey Patient Bill of Rights, adopted in the late 1980s.[76] Patients rights include, but are not limited to, the right of access to care; the right to be treated without discrimination; the right to be introduced to any healthcare provider by name in addition to the use of a name badge; the right to receive confidential treatment; the right to personal medical records and the procedure for gaining access to them; the right to give informed consent; the right to refuse medical care with knowledge of the consequences; the right to decline participation in medical research or medical training; the right to be informed of the facility's policies and procedures regarding the withdrawal and withholding of life support; and the right to be informed of the entitlement to have care transferred from a practitioner or facility and the procedure to accomplish this.

The New Jersey Patient Bill of Rights provides a strongly visible public commitment by all the parties concerned regarding the rights of the patients it serves. This, coupled with an accessible and enforceable mechanism of redress for patients who feel they may have been wronged or had their rights violated, signifies that the strategy is working. The Bill expresses a strong, universal commitment to the rights of all patients, and this has resulted in further advocating for individuals with special needs or challenges. For example, deaf patients must be provided with their preferred means of communication.[77]

In October 1997, the US state of Oregon legalized physician-assisted suicide (PAS). Since then, many states have rejected assisted suicide measures – some of them multiple times – whereas the states of Washington, Vermont, New Mexico and Montana all legalized PAS between 1997 and 2013. California might soon be added to the list: California senators gave final approval on a 23–14 vote after an emotional debate on 11 September 2015 to a PAS bill that would allow terminally ill patients to legally end their lives. The measure faces an uncertain future because the Governor might not sign the act. The measure to allow doctors to prescribe life-ending medication succeeded on its second attempt; it includes requirements that the patient be physically capable of taking the medication themselves, that two doctors approve it, that the patient sub-mit several written requests, and that there be two witnesses.[78] In the US states that have legalized PAS, only residents of those states are allowed access to legal suicide assistance.

Euthanasia remains illegal in all US States.[79] Debates about euthanasia raged in the United States at the turn of the nineteenth century, which resulted in an 1906 Ohio bill to legalize euthanasia that was ultimately defeated.[80] Euthanasia advocacy in the US peaked again during the 1930s, only to diminish significantly during and after World War II. Euthanasia efforts were revived during the 1960s and 1970s under the right-to-die rubric, physician-assisted death in liberal bioethics, and through advance directives and do-not-resuscitate orders. The inflammatory nature of US debates on the subject has highlighted the biggest cultural barrier to delivering palliative and hospice care – the fact that people associate such care with dying rather than with providing quality of life when suffering terminal illness. Proponents of euthanasia have presented four main arguments:[81]

- to recognize a right to self-determination, allowing to choose one's own fate;
- to assist patients to die might be a better choice than requiring that they continue to suffer;
- to distinguish between euthanasia and withdrawal or withholding treatment;
- to reassure that permitting euthanasia will not necessarily lead to unacceptable consequences.

In the US, discussion of end-of-life care often inflames religious sentiment that holds the sanctity of life paramount. The issue is complicated by the perception that hospice care is often associated with giving up. Opponents to a legal right to euthanasia or assisted suicide typically appeal to three arguments: a 'slippery slope' argument (society will be inexorably led to permit further unethical actions); an argument about the dangers of practising euthanasia beyond the tight boundaries established by the law; and the above mentioned argument about the sacred and non-disposable value of human life. Elisabeth Kübler-Ross, an eminent Swiss-American psychiatrist, opposed euthanasia in her seminal book, *On Death and Dying And The Five Stages of Grief* (1969) and encouraged the hospice care movement, believing that euthanasia would prevent people from completing their 'unfinished business'.[82]

Cost of palliative care
Financial concerns can be a major burden for many patients and families facing a terminal illness. The federal administration exercises a large financial role through Medicare, a national social insurance programme that provides health insurance for Americans aged 65 and older who have

worked and paid into the system. The federal administration sets standards for Medicare providers and determines what drugs may be sold, while the insurance industry and health codes are regulated at state or local level. Medicaid, a social healthcare programme for families and individuals with low income and limited resources, also funds end-of-life care. It is jointly paid for by the state and federal governments and managed by the states. In addition to Medicare and Medicaid, most private insurance plans cover hospice care.

The Medicare Hospice Benefit[83] enacted by Congress in 1982 is the predominate source of payment for hospice care. In 2012, 83.7 per cent of hospice patients were covered by the Medicare Hospice Benefit. Other payment sources are the Medicaid Hospice Benefit,[84] the Health Maintenance Organization,[85] other managed care organizations and most private health insurance plans. If patients do not have insurance or their insurance does not cover hospice care, they are still entitled to contact a hospice. However, those not yet eligible for Medicare and not sufficiently poor to qualify for Medicaid must either rely on private health insurance, convert their life insurance policies to help pay for hospice treatment, or find other sources of funding. While each hospice has its own policies concerning payment, it is a hospice tradition to offer services based on need rather than on the ability to pay.[86]

Estimates show that about 27 per cent of Medicare's annual budget ($88 billion out of a total $327 billion in 2006) goes to care for patients in their final year of life.[87] A well-established network of non-profit hospices in the US plays an important role in cutting National Health Service expenditure.

Canada

Background

Palliative care was introduced in Canada forty years ago to meet the needs of people with an incurable disease that seriously compromised their survival.[88] It evolved following a unique care philosophy that takes a holistic approach, offering new outlooks and including a series of measures to humanize care for end-of-life patients and their families.

Canada has set up a national strategy on palliative and end-of-life care,[89] but one weakness in its provincially administered universal healthcare system is the lack of a nationwide standard for palliative care,[90] which generates non-homogeneous approaches and different levels of provision across the country.[91] Although Canada is geographically large, it has a population of fewer than 34 million people: hospice and palliative care services reflect the size of the population, yet they cannot cover the entire country.

The Canadian Palliative Care Association reaffirms the values intended to guide palliative care services:[92]

- The intrinsic value of each person as a unique individual, the value of life, and the inescapable nature of death.
- The necessary participation of patients through their free and informed consent to ensure they are party to decisions in accordance with their wishes on all matters concerning them, including their true condition, and that their choices are respected.
- The duty of confidentiality on the part of caregivers, which prevents the release of personal information without patient authorization.
- The right to compassionate caregiver services respectful of what provides meaning to people's lives — their values, culture, beliefs, and religious practices and those of their families.

Like many Western societies, the Canadian population will age quickly in the coming decades. For example, the number of people aged 65 or over, which was 13 per cent in 2001, will reach 25 per cent in 2036 and 30 per cent in 2041. This fact will have sizeable repercussions on the health and social services needs of end-of-life patients.

This trend will lead to an increase in the number of people with progressive and often chronic diseases that require end-of-life palliative care. Canadian society is faced with the challenge of dealing with a large number of deaths in a very short period of time, with all the resulting psychological and social consequences.

Palliative care services and hospice care

In 1975, a palliative care unit was opened at the St Boniface Hospital in Winnipeg, Manitoba, and weeks later, in 1976, a similar palliative care unit was opened at the Royal Victoria Hospital in Montreal, Quebec, by doctor Balfour Mount. Dr Mount, a pioneer in hospice/palliative care, introduced the term 'palliative care' rather than 'hospice' because in Canadian historical culture the word hospice was commonly associated with a place of last resort for the poor or derelict. In 1976 the First International Congress on the Care of the Terminally Ill was held in Montreal, and was organized thereafter every two years by doctor Mount and his colleagues.

Canada continues to be a leader in hospice/palliative care, in part because of a strong policy framework that has underpinned the development of services, and the environment within which those services operate.

The Palliative Care Foundation in Toronto, Ontario, released an official definition of hospice palliative care in 1981, stating that, 'Palliative care is active compassionate care of the terminally ill at a time when their disease is no longer responsive to traditional treatment aimed at cure and prolongation of life and when the control of symptoms, physical and emotional, is paramount. It is multidisciplinary in its approach and encompasses the patient, the family and the community in its scope.' Two years later, the University of Ottawa, Ontario created Canada's first university institute for research and education in palliative care. The Canadian Palliative Care Association was established in November 1991 and opened its first office in Ottawa in February 1994. The organization later changed its name to the Canadian Hospice Palliative Care Association

(CHPCA), due to hospice care and palliative care being recognized as one and the same. Since 1981, the British Columbia Ministry of Health has supported a community palliative care project, starting with an inpatient unit at the Royal Jubilee Hospital in Victoria, BC, and the second unit at Vancouver, BC, General Hospital. The BC Ministry of Health has also provided home care support to enable terminally ill patients to remain in the comfort of their own homes. However, in general, hospice programmes must raise their own funds in their communities to financially support their individual programmes.

Where palliative care is provided

In Canada, due to the tendency to prefer home death, health system restructuring has led to a greater focus on home-based palliative care as an alternative to institutionalized palliative care.

Palliative care is offered in various organizational settings:

- Community based hospice palliative care
  This type of programme has no special facility of its own other than an office. The programme centres around the patient, whether they are at home or in a healthcare facility. A multidiscipline team approach is used to provide physical, emotional and spiritual support for the patient and the family.
- Hospital based
  A unit within the hospital is specifically allocated for terminally ill patients to die in if they so choose, as well as for symptom management and respite. The unit may have either a totally independent staff or personnel who rotate from the main hospital.
- Hospital-based team
  This team has no designated place within the hospital, but there will be a specific number of designated beds scattered throughout the hospital to be used for palliative care patients. Patient care is administered by the regular ward staff, and the team sees the patient on a daily basis, making suggestions for care as they assess the needs.

- Hospice Bed
    This is a bed designated in a location elsewhere than a hospital. The multidisciplinary team used for the community base is utilized here as well.
- Free-standing hospice
    The free-standing hospice is housed in its own building and served by a multidisciplinary team.

The Canadian Hospice Palliative Care Association (CHPCA) publishes online the *Canadian Directory of Hospice Palliative Care Services*.[93] This online directory has been designed to provide Canadian citizens with information on the availability of hospice palliative care services across Canada. The directory provides a province-by-province listing of programmes and services, contact information for these, and where they provide care. The International Association for Hospice & Palliative Care (IAHPC) publishes online a *Global Directory of Palliative Care Services, Hospices and Organizations*, where citizens can find information on palliative care service providers associations and umbrella organizations. Such information is gathered by IAHPC from voluntary submissions from the service providers' organizations.[94]

Legal aspects

In federal Canada, euthanasia at the time of writing is illegal and is considered as murder. Suicide is not a crime in Canada and has not been such since 1972, but physician-assisted suicide *is* illegal. In February 2015 a decision by the Supreme Court of Canada struck down the provision prohibiting assisted suicide, though the ruling does not take effect until 2016.[95]

However a new law decriminalizing euthanasia (Bill 52, 'An Act respecting end-of-life care')[96] is due to come into force on 10 December 2015 in Quebec, unless the federal government challenges it. Bill 52 was passed in June 2014 in the Quebec National Assembly in a 94–22 free vote. The purpose of this Act is to ensure that end-of-life patients are provided care that is respectful of their dignity and their autonomy, and to recognize the primacy of wishes expressed freely and clearly with respect to end-of-life care. It sets out special rules applicable to the providers of end-of-life care; that is, institutions, palliative care hospices and private health facilities, in order to provide a framework for the organization and regulation of end-of-life care. In this respect, it specifies the special functions and powers of health and social services agencies and of the Quebec Minister of Health and Social Services. It also establishes specific requirements for certain types of end-of-life care: namely, continuous palliative sedation and medical aid in dying. The latter is in fact euthanasia, although this word is not mentioned in the text of the Act. Medical aid in dying is defined as 'care consisting in the administration by a physician of medications or substances to an end-of-life patient, at the patient's request, in order to relieve their suffering by hastening death'. The Act prescribes the criteria that must be met for a person to obtain medical aid in dying and the requirements to be complied with before a physician may administer it.

A commission on end-of-life care has been established under the title *Commission sur les soins de fin de vie* [Commission on end-of-life care], as well as rules with respect to its composition and operations. The mandate of the Commission is to examine all matters relating to end-of-life care, and to oversee the application of specific requirements relating to medical aid in dying.

The Act establishes an advance medical directives regime and specifies the conditions that must be met in order for such directives to have binding force.

Cost of palliative care

In the current environment of rising healthcare costs and concerns about the sustainability of publicly funded healthcare, policymakers are paying more attention to the costs associated with the final year of life. The cost of dying in Canada incurred by the healthcare institutions ranges from as low as $10,000 for a sudden death to between $30,000 and $40,000 for someone with a terminal disease such as cancer or chronic obstructive pulmonary disease. The cost of dying varies not only by cause but also by where people die: on average it costs $36,000 to die in a chronic care facility, compared to $16,000 to die at home.[97] This is due to changes in the distribution of costs borne by different stakeholders, whereas the estimated total societal cost of end-of-life care shows no significant difference because hospitalization costs for hospital-death patients were replaced by higher, unpaid caregiver time, and outpatient service costs for home-death patients.[98] Developing better palliative and home care services could significantly reduce overall societal costs.[99]

Most of these end-of-life costs are absorbed by the healthcare system, although families also experience substantial caregiving and out-of-pocket costs. Hospice palliative care services can reduce the costs of dying and improve patient care. They can significantly reduce the healthcare costs of patients who are dying by reducing hospital admissions, the length of hospital stays, re-admissions, visits to intensive care units, and inappropriate diagnostics or interventions.

Hospital-based palliative care reduces the cost of end-of-life care by 50 per cent or more in comparison to the cost of care provided in conventional internal medical wards. Primarily, this is done by reducing the number of intensive care unit admissions, diagnostic testing, interventional procedures and overall hospital length of stay.

In 2012, only 16-30 per cent of Canadians had access to or received hospice palliative and end-of-life care. Three-quarters of deaths still occur in hospitals and long-term care facilities rather than taking place at home, which most Canadians would prefer. Improved and more equitable access to hospice palliative care could not only save the Canadian healthcare system millions of dollars each year but also enhance care and quality of life for patients and families.

Ireland

Background

As early as the twelfth century, monastic societies founded hospitals within their walls to care for the sick. Communities outside cloister walls imitated this and built hospitals. As science and medicine developed further, especially anatomy and surgery, care began to concentrate on cure. However, monks and nuns continued to care for those for whom cure was not an option. Sister Mary Aikenhead (1787–1858) from Cork, Ireland, founder of the Congregation of the Religious Sisters of Charity, opened Our Lady's Hospice (1845) as a charitable and religious mission to care for those dying of tuberculosis and living in poverty. The Congregation established Our Lady's Hospice in Harold's Cross, Dublin, in 1879. New buildings were added, including a night school for women and girls and a Sunday school. Throughout the twentieth century there were further developments, including palliative care facilities for the hospice.

Palliative care services and hospice care

Palliative care is provided in Ireland by the Health Service Executive Ireland (HSE), to people of any age and at any stage of their illness, in order to better manage symptoms and complications when undergoing, for example, treatments such as chemotherapy. Each healthcare team has three levels of palliative care provision representing increasing specialization:

Level 1: in any location or setting all healthcare professionals, as part of their role, use a palliative care approach.
Level 2: in any location, healthcare professionals with additional and specialized know-how practise a palliative care approach.
Level 3: in a hospice or specialized hospital ward, healthcare professionals with extensive knowledge and skills work solely in palliative care.

The hospice is a specialist unit that provides palliative care. There are ten inpatient hospices in Ireland offering inpatient or outpatient day care. The hospice mainly treats patients with illnesses that cannot be cured. Many people who receive hospice care have cancer, but hospices also treat patients with other conditions. Patients are referred to the hospice as inpatients for the following reasons:

- To control symptoms: for example, pain or nausea.
- To provide temporary respite for patients and their carers.
- For rehabilitation purposes. Services such as physiotherapy, occupational therapy, complementary therapies and dietetics may be available to assist in improving patients' well-being and quality of life.
- For end-of-life care.

Where care is provided

It is important to enable people to die where they prefer. Patients most commonly express a wish to die at home, but in addition to preference, a number of factors also influence the place of death. When a seriously ill, hospitalized patient does express a wish to die at home their request is not simply viewed as impractical or impossible. Rather, a realistic evaluation of the feasibility of different options is undertaken. The HSE facilitates this by promoting collaborative working and effective communication across primary and secondary care to ensure a safe, smooth and seamless transition of care from hospital to community for patients with terminal illnesses who choose to be cared for in their own home during their last days of life.

Palliative care can be arranged by the family doctor (GP) or by the hospital the patient is attending. Palliative care is provided in the following settings:[100]

- General hospitals, by the specialist palliative care team.
- A person's own home, by specialist palliative care nurses who work with the patient's family doctor, the specialist palliative care team and the public health nurse.
- Community hospitals and nursing homes, by specialist palliative nurses who work with the patient's family doctor and/or a specialist palliative care team.
- The Inpatient hospices.

Citizens seeking to arrange palliative care can call the free phone number (1800 200 700) and speak in confidence to a specialist nurse.

Legal aspects

Both euthanasia and assisted suicide are illegal under Irish law. Depending on the circumstances, euthanasia is regarded as either manslaughter or murder and is punishable by sentences up to life imprisonment.

It is not, however, illegal to remove life support or to withhold or withdraw other treatment, should a person or their next of kin request it. A September 2010 *Irish Times* poll showed that a majority of 57 per cent of adults believed that physician-assisted suicide should be legal for terminally ill patients who request it.[101]

In Ireland, there is no legislation which provides for the recognition and enforcement of an advance care directive, also known as a 'living will', which is a statement about the type and extent of medical or surgical treatment patients may or may not want in the future on the assumption that they might not be able to make that decision for themselves at the relevant time. This does not necessarily mean that these advance care directives are not valid, but it does mean that information and guidance from other jurisdictions might not apply.

Patients cannot give anyone else any legal right to make decisions on their behalf about their healthcare, should they be incapable of doing so themselves, but they may suggest to their doctor or hospital that the wishes of certain people should be taken into account. However, they cannot be assured that the doctor or hospital will abide by their wishes.

If a healthcare issue arises and the patient is incapable of making a decision, it is the practice to consult with next of kin. It is not clear what legal basis supports this, given that next of kin have no right to make decisions on behalf of adults. Medical ethics currently in force in Ireland state that consultation with next of kin is desirable if the patient is unable to make a decision or to communicate, and it provides for a second opinion if there is a difference of opinion between the patient's family and the doctor. Next of kin are (in order) spouse, children, parents and siblings. Partners have no legal status and may even experience difficulties in visiting patients if family members object. This is the case whether the patient is in either a heterosexual or a homosexual relationship.[102]

Cost of palliative care

In Ireland, everyone is entitled to public hospital care. Despite this, the number of citizens purchasing private health insurance has continued to grow to the point that about 40 per cent of the population now has private health insurance. This is due to perceived concerns (often unfounded) about waiting times for public care and the quality of that care.[103] The cost of supplying palliative care in Ireland is on a par with care provided in comparable acute settings; the average yearly hospice bed cost for 2010 was €262,000, or €718 per day for specialist inpatient units, while the average cost of an acute hospital bed was €909 per day.[104]

The delivery of palliative care services in Ireland is heavily reliant on the voluntary sector. As an example, Galway Hospice Foundation is a voluntary organization established in 1986.[105] It has been awarded accreditation by Caspe Healthcare Knowledge Systems and received ISO 9001:2008 certification. The Galway Hospice depends on the generosity and goodwill of the public to fund the Home Care Service (available 7 days a week, 365 days a year), Day Care Service, Bereavement Support Service and Educational Facility. Altogether, the provision of these services costs in excess of €1.6 million per annum.

While the majority of patients cared for by the Galway Hospice team express the wish to remain at home, and with the support of the Home Care Service are able to do so, there are patients who, for a variety of reasons, cannot. Some patients' symptoms may be difficult to control in the community, carers may need a period of respite, and sometimes patients may not have adequate support systems to allow them to remain in their own homes throughout their illness.

In order to meet the needs of such patients, in 1992 the Galway Hospice Foundation set about raising the capital cost for a purpose-built facility incorporating inpatient, day care and support services. The cost, which was approximately €2.6 million (a very sizeable sum at that time), was raised solely through voluntary donations from the community, businesses, the farming and professional sectors of Galway city and county, and individual donations from far and wide.

In 1997, funding from the Western Health Board (now HSE West) was approved for the running costs of the Inpatient Unit, allowing the first patients to be admitted in December of that year. Patients are admitted for symptom control, respite, psychological support and end-of-life care, or a combination of these. The usual length of stay is approximately two weeks.

When Irish citizens with a cancer diagnosis experience financial difficulty, yet find themselves unable to benefit for whatever reason from schemes such as social welfare support, they may apply to Financial Aid, a hardship fund set up by the Irish Cancer Society to help patients and their families in covering costs they cannot face, such as home heating, child care or respite.

Australia

Background

Healthcare in Australia is provided by both the government and private institutions. The Federal Minister for Health administers national health policy, elements of which are operated by individual state governments. Australia is a high-income country, and this is reflected by the population's general good status of health. Life expectancy in Australia is among the highest in the world. Despite this high standard of health, certain disparities in the Australian healthcare system are a problem. The poor, those living in remote areas and the indigenous population are, in general, less healthy than the rest. The Australian Institute of Health and Welfare noted that compared with the inhabitants of major cities, people in regional and remote areas were less likely to report excellent or very good health, with life expectancy decreasing with increasing remoteness. Programmes have been implemented to reduce this gap. These include increased outreach to the indigenous communities and government subsidies to provide services for people in remote or rural areas, and for people belonging to non-English-speaking groups.[106] A desire to educate the community about palliative care falters at the doorstep of non-English-speaking groups. The inability of some Australians to read English is merely the first stumbling block. Cultural attitudes and traditions create a tricky path, requiring delicate steps. The fact that the words death, dying and cancer are taboo for many cultures creates immediate difficulties in discussing palliative care.[107]

With regard to end-of-life care, the situation in Australia presents a number of differences across geographical areas, given that the institutions of the various Australian states can legislate autonomously on these matters. Territories are in a different position. Unlike the states, which are sovereign entities possessing legislative power in their own right, a territory's legislative power is derived through a grant issued by the Commonwealth Parliament, which still retains the power – in practice very rarely exercised – to legislate for the territory. The level of end-of-life care is, nevertheless, at the highest level of world standards throughout the country.

Whilst there is a National Palliative Care Programme that supports national approaches, most palliative care service provision occurs within the remit of the state and territory health systems. Each state and territory has an articulated approach to palliative care in its jurisdiction. The National Palliative Care Strategy is intended to provide the framework for the Commonwealth, states and territories to work together cooperatively and collaboratively.[108]

Different service sectors adhere to a number of distinct definitions for palliative care. The Commonwealth recognizes that state and territory jurisdictions work under varying definitions. Each regional jurisdiction has articulated its definition in its strategic documents. The Palliative Care Intergovernmental Forum adopted the WHO definition reported earlier in this appendix as the national definition of palliative care.

Palliative care services and hospice care

Palliative care usually consists of medication and treatments, medical reviews and assessments, help and guidance with accessing information and resources, short-term care relief and respite care, counselling and emotional support, and bereavement support for carers and family after a patient's death. Palliative Care Australia, the national organization representing all state and territory palliative care organizations, says that a palliative approach is used by primary care services and practitioners to improve the quality of life for individuals with a life-limiting illness, and for their caregivers and family. The palliative approach incorporates a concern for the holistic needs of patients and caregivers, which is reflected in the assessment process, in the primary treatment of pain, and in the provision of physical, psychological, social and spiritual care. Application of the palliative approach to the care of an individual is not delayed until the final stages of their illness. Instead, it provides a focus on active, comfort-oriented care and a positive approach to reducing suffering and promoting understanding of loss and bereavement in the wider community. Underlying the philosophy of a palliative approach is the view that death, dying and bereavement are all an integral part of life.

Over the last twenty years in Australia, the palliative care specialization has advanced considerably.[109] A global comparative study of end-of-life care conducted by the Economist Intelligence Unit gave the highest ratings to Australia (and the UK) out of 40 countries studied.[110] The two countries received a rating of 7.9 out of 10 in an analysis of access to services, quality of care and public awareness.

The idea of a good death held by hospice and palliative care practitioners is changing in Australia. Palliative care practitioners are searching for an ideology to inform their practice within the context of a complex society for which there is no 'one' good death, reflecting the uncertainties held by many Australians. The good death ideology of the original hospice movement proposed a manner of dying in which open communication and acceptance of death were actively encouraged. This model, however, has become increasingly inappropriate in the current climate of patient autonomy and consumer choice. A practice of palliative care, which follows the ethic of individual choice, has emerged from and replaced the original hospice movement.[111]

Within Australia, palliative care is provided across the health and human services spectrum by public hospitals, private hospitals, hospices, general practitioners, justice health services, disability services and specialist palliative care services – both public and private – in inpatient as well as community-based settings. Specialist palliative care services operate from a variety of settings, including specialist inpatient consulting services, specialist inpatient settings, hospices and community-based specialist services. Specialist palliative care comes into play when people experience severe or complex problems as their condition advances. These individuals can then be referred to a specialist palliative care service where a team of specialist professionals will work to meet their needs. Alternatively, general practitioners may seek advice from specialist palliative care services on their patients' behalf.

Where care is provided

Hospices and palliative care services for inpatients and patients at home are available nationwide. Some of these services are offered by non-profit organizations. Palliative care service provision occurs within the remit of the state and territory health systems. For information on who to contact regarding palliative care service provision in a particular area, the patient's family can consult a GP, hospital or health centre for more specialized support, or visit the National Palliative Care Service Directory online.[112]

The Australian Government also provides information on what to do following a death, including information about financial matters, who to notify, and relevant payments and services.

Remaining at home is the preferred choice of most people when they age and most healthy Australians, when asked where they would prefer to die, nominate their home as their wish. Help is provided for older adults to either stay at home or to be discharged as soon as possible from hospital or rehabilitation beds. For the infirm, living at home may necessitate safety and convenience measures, such as making bathrooms accessible and safe, fitting stair lifts and placing handrails in corridors. Living at home is made easier by the Community Support Services, which offer meals, social and transportation services, adult day care, Senior Centres, personal home-care services and nursing care.

However, the statistics on place of death indicate that a home death is relatively uncommon; only 16 per cent of people die at home. Twenty per cent of people die in hospices and 10 per cent in nursing homes. The rest die in hospitals. This results in a high financial burden on the health system and a potentially poorer quality of death.

Legal aspects

Currently, euthanasia and physician-assisted suicide are illegal in Australia; to assist with euthanasia is also a crime, although prosecutions have been rare. The closest euthanasia has come to being legalized by a state was in Tasmania in 2013 when an Australian Greens party voluntary euthanasia bill was narrowly defeated in the Tasmanian House of Assembly by a vote of 13 to 12.

Euthanasia and physician-assisted suicide had previously been legalized in Australia's Northern Territory by the Rights of the Terminally Ill Act, approved by the NT Parliament in 1995, at a time when no such bill had been adopted anywhere else in the world. The act allowed, under strict conditions, terminally ill patients to commit physician-assisted suicide or ask for euthanasia, either by the procurement of drugs or by the direct involvement of a physician administering the lethal substance to the patient.[113] It required a somewhat lengthy application process, designed to ensure that patients were both mentally competent to make the decision and in fact terminally ill. It passed by a vote of 15 to 10 during the year 1995 and came into force in July 1996. Only nine months later, in March 1997, the law was voided by the federal Euthanasia Laws Act 1997.[114] However, four people had already died under the legislation through physician-assisted suicide.[115] The law had applied to all Australian citizens, and one resident from South Australia did take advantage of it.

The Euthanasia Laws Act 1997 has no effect on the power of an Australian state to pass any law permitting euthanasia, and it expressly leaves open the possibility of a territory passing laws regarding the withholding of life support.

Public debates held about euthanasia and physician-assisted suicide raised awareness and gained strong media attention. Pressure brought on policymakers over these issues has been a catalyst for the improvement of palliative care services. In fact, the federal overturning of the NT euthanasia law of 1996 led to increased national funding for end-of-life care.

Advance Health Directives are legal documents in Western Australia and in other states and territories. With Advance Health Directives, capable adults can set out their decisions about what kind of treatments they agree or do not agree to, including withholding or withdrawing life-sustaining treatments and artificial feeding. An Advance Health Directive can come into effect if, later on, the person is no longer able to make competent judgements about their treatment. Advance Care Planning also includes communicating an individual's views, preferences and decisions about their future care, such as where they would like to be cared for when dying, and what kind of funeral would they prefer.

Guidelines for withholding and/or withdrawing life-sustaining measures, including artificial feeding, have been produced by several states.[116] These identify principles that apply to decision-making and quality care at the end of life, and focus on considerations about ethical and special matters, such as decision-making for people who are incapable of deciding for themselves.

Cost of palliative care

Healthcare in Australia is universal. In 1988, palliative care was enshrined in the Australian healthcare agreements, through which the federal government funds expenditures on behalf of the country's states and territories. In the financial year 2011–2012, the national health system was financed at 9.5 per cent of GDP. The federal government pays a large percentage of the cost of services in public hospitals, typically covering 100 per cent of in-hospital costs, 75 per cent of general practitioner costs and 85 per cent of specialist services. Most home care is government funded. Under the Original Medicare Safety Net, once the annual threshold of patient out-of-pocket expenses for non-hospital Medicare services has been reached, the Medicare benefit is increased to 100 per cent (up from 85 per cent) for the remainder of the calendar year. The Extended Medicare Safety Net, introduced in 2004, provides an additional payment for non-hospital Medicare services once an annual threshold of patient spending is reached. Out-of-pocket costs represent the difference between the Medicare payment for treatment and the fee the practitioner charges the patient. Once patients' out-of-pocket threshold is reached, for the remainder of the calendar year they receive 80 per cent of out-of-pocket costs in addition to the standard Medicare payment.

Medicare, instituted in 1984, is the publicly funded universal healthcare system in Australia. It coexists alongside a private health system. Medicare is funded partly by an income tax surcharge known as the Medicare Levy, which is currently set at 2 per cent of a person's taxable income (with exceptions for low-income earners), with the balance provided by the government from general revenue. An additional levy of 1 per cent is imposed on high-income earners without private health insurance. As well as Medicare, there is a separate Pharmaceutical Benefits Scheme that considerably subsidizes a range of prescription medications.

In circumstances where the government pays a large subsidy on costs, the patient pays the remainder unless the provider of the service decides otherwise and leaves the patient with nothing to pay. The Australian Government's Department of Human Services delivers a range of payments and services supporting people in need. Such provisions include respite services, which assist families in caring for family members with physical disabilities, thus enabling them to stay together as a unit.

Where a particular service is not covered, patients must pay the full amount unless they hold a Low Income Earner card, which may entitle them to subsidized access. Individuals can take out private health insurance to cover out-of-pocket costs, subscribing either to a plan that covers certain selected services or to a full coverage plan. The Australian government has introduced a number of incentives to encourage adults to take out private hospital insurance.

New Zealand

Background

Palliative care is a crucial part of New Zealand's healthcare system, providing care and support for people with life-limiting illnesses and their families. It is expected that the need for palliative care will grow and it is considered important that health professionals and the New Zealanders they serve understand what it entails and how it can benefit patients and their families. New Zealand is the third best place in the world to die — just behind the United Kingdom and Australia, according to the Economist Intelligence Unit.[117] This is a reflection of the quality of care available for people at the end of life, and the cost and availability of that care.

Following an extensive consultation and analysis initiated in 1997, in 2001 the New Zealand Palliative Care Strategy set in place a systematic and informed approach to the provision and funding of palliative care services.[118]

The current New Zealand Government is concerned to ensure that all people who are dying, and their families, have access to palliative care services that are provided in a coordinated and culturally appropriate way. For this reason it has committed additional funding to ensure that this strategy can begin to be implemented immediately. The strategy recommends that palliative care should be generally available to people whose death from progressive disease is likely to occur within one year. An increasing number of New Zealanders are in need of palliative care services: the proportion of the population aged 65 or over is projected to more than double (from 12 per cent up to 26 per cent) over the next 50 years.

Government expenditure (GGE) in New Zealand is 40 per cent of GDP. Twenty per cent of GGE is spent on health. The New Zealand government supports 83 per cent of health care costs while households spend 11 per cent. Funding resources from the Ministry of Health are devolved to the District Health Boards (DHBs), which run and own public hospitals. Their objectives are to ensure accessible and appropriate services for people from lower socio-economic groups; to establish accessible and appropriate services for Mäori and Pacific populations; and to ensure that the terminally ill and their families receive services when the former are discharged from hospital.

New Zealand has a mix of public and private hospitals, but public hospitals dominate hospital care, including virtually all emergency care.

The Government's vision in implementing the strategy is that all people who are terminally ill and could benefit from palliative care should have timely access to quality palliative care services that are culturally appropriate to the people they serve. Thus the government is committed to: ensuring that at least one local palliative care service is available for each DHB; developing specialist palliative care services; implementing hospital palliative care teams and ensuring their lifelong training; developing quality requirements for palliative care services; informing the public about palliative care services; and addressing issues of income support.

Palliative care services and hospice care

It should be pointed out that in New Zealand the term 'hospice' has more than one meaning. It is used to refer to not only residential healthcare homes for the elderly at the end of their lives, but also to the concept and methods of palliative care for both inpatients and outpatients.

Palliative care is recognized nationwide as a legitimate component of healthcare and it is not delivered solely by hospices. It is also provided by GPs, district nurses, in residential care facilities and in hospitals. Over 700 doctors, nurses and healthcare professionals provide palliative care services in New Zealand, while 7,000 volunteers (out of a population of four million) deliver hospice services totalling 480,000 hours a year.

Palliative care in New Zealand arose within local communities in order to provide holistic care for adults with terminal cancer through the support of local funding and volunteers. The starting point for hospice care is the acceptance of the reality of death. Death is not an illness requiring treatment but the end of life's journey, which requires adequate pain relief, holistic care and compassionate assistance. Assuring quality care for the terminally ill and support for their families is considered essential for the future well-being of New Zealand society.

Palliative care is intended for people who are dying from active, progressive diseases or other conditions that are not responsive to curative treatment. Palliative care embraces the physical, social, emotional and spiritual elements of well-being and enhances a person's quality of life while they are dying. Palliative care services are generally provided by a multidisciplinary team that works with the dying person and provides support for their family. Palliative care affirms life and regards dying as a normal process; it neither hastens nor postpones death. It aims to provide relief from distressing symptoms, and integrates physical, social, emotional and spiritual aspects of care to help the dying and their family attain an acceptable quality of life. It offers help to the family carers during the person's illness and the family's bereavement.

There are a number of factors preventing delivery of the best palliative care, among them a lack of recognition that people affected by conditions other than cancer can benefit from palliative care services, a lack of workforce planning for palliative care, and variability in the funding of palliative care services.

Modern hospices in New Zealand can be traced back to the model of St Christopher's Hospice, inspired by the charisma and skill of Dame Cicely Saunders and her unique zeal in promoting the concept of hospice care internationally. Twelve years after the opening of St Christopher's Hospice in London, in June 1979, New Zealand's first hospice, Mary Potter Hospice, was opened in Wellington. Later that year, Te Omanga Hospice opened in Lower Hutt, and St Joseph's Mercy Hospice in Auckland.[119] Increasingly, hospices have become associated as places where people die, but such a notion is impoverishing. In New Zealand today, a hospice is regarded primarily as the manifestation of a concept of care, or a philosophy of care. Initially, hospice programmes emphasized inpatient care of the terminally ill: patients were admitted to a residential facility where they received comfort and care from an attentive, multidisciplinary team of caregivers until they died. Hospice programmes now primarily provide a wide range of residential and home-based services, together with a day centre where patients who live at home are able to come to be assessed, receive counselling, advice, engage in activities and have companionship. From small beginnings the hospice movement in New Zealand has now developed into forty-two hospice programmes. A key goal of the hospice movement is its educational role for the medical and nursing professions and wider community.

Hospice New Zealand is a national hospice body that promotes hospice and palliative care.[120] It is actively involved in research and education, workforce development, establishing standards of healthcare, providing information and advice to hospices, stakeholders and the general public, and helping and supporting hospices nationwide.

Where care is provided

Currently New Zealand has four hospital-based palliative care teams; these are located in Auckland, Waikato, Christchurch and Wellington. DHBs will set up hospital palliative care teams in locations where they are currently lacking.

Throughout the country, palliative care services are provided in inpatient centres and at patients' homes. They support the choice to die at home since research shows that 50–70 per cent of people would prefer home care. Information on services provided is available at the URLs of hospices located in each geographical area.[121]

Each of the hospices offers a number of palliative care services. For example, Amitabha Hospice Service at Forrest Hill, Auckland, provides hospice volunteer caregiver support in all suburbs of greater Auckland. Following the WHO guidelines for palliative care and the New Zealand Palliative Care Strategy, the Amitabha Hospice provides free practical help and companionship for those with progressive degenerative conditions or terminal illness through the aid of specially trained volunteers, thus improving the quality of life of patients and their families. By bringing compassionate care into the individual's home with multicultural and multilingual staff and volunteers, Amitabha caregivers offer people the option of remaining in their own homes. Services provided include pastoral care from qualified practitioners for people of all spiritual beliefs, and the provision of relaxation, meditation, massage, reiki and stress management treatments. Amitabha Hospice caregivers offer free assistance at home by giving practical help where appropriate, such as doing shopping, making light meals, giving massages and teaching relaxation and meditation techniques. They offer respite to the usual caregiver or family member, enabling the latter to have 'time out' to rest, work, do errands or simply take a break.

Legal aspects

In New Zealand, the question of legalizing euthanasia and/or physician-assisted suicide (PAS) is an ongoing debate. Discussions about euthanasia often arise in the media in response to high profile court cases, whether national or foreign, or when there are visits to New Zealand by individuals promoting euthanasia or speaking against it.

In 2015, a lawyer who was suffering from a terminal brain cancer sought a High Court ruling to confirm that assisted dying was not unlawful under the Crimes Act, and that a ban on assisted dying contravened her human rights under the New Zealand Bill of Rights Act. The Court found that assisted dying was unlawful and that the relevant provisions of the Crimes Act were consistent with the rights and freedoms contained in the Bill of Rights Act. It further suggested that changes to the law could only be made by Parliament. Following this ruling, a petition organized by the Voluntary Euthanasia Society was presented to Parliament in June 2015. It asked that the House of Representatives investigate public attitudes towards the introduction of legislation permitting medically assisted dying.

Many people see this issue primarily as a debate about freedom of choice. The opponents to euthanasia consider that a change in the law would pose real dangers for New Zealand's society, and from the experience in other countries they fear that, in spite of lawmakers' best intentions, there would be no adequate legal safeguards to protect vulnerable groups such as children, the elderly, or those with disabilities should euthanasia or PAS be legalized.[122]

Hospice New Zealand does not support a change in the law to legalize assisted dying in any form. Nor does it consider that a change in the law would be in the best interests of the people they care for. The whole ethos of hospice and palliative care as defined by the WHO is that it 'intends neither to hasten nor postpone death'.

Cost of palliative care

All of New Zealand's four million residents have access to a broad range of health and disability services with substantive government funding. The publicly funded system covers public health preventive and promotional services, inpatient and outpatient hospital care, primary health care services, inpatient and outpatient prescription drugs, mental healthcare, dental care for school children, and disability support services. Residents have free choice of a GP. Healthcare is mostly free for children under age six, and is subsidized to a significant degree for all people enrolled with Primary Health Organizations, which includes 95 per cent of the public.

Not-for-profit insurers generally cover private medical care. Private insurance is most commonly used to cover cost-sharing requirements, elective surgery in private hospitals, and specialist outpatient consultations. About one-third of New Zealanders have some form of private health insurance.

Patients are billed co-payments for pharmaceuticals, private hospital or specialist care, and adult dental care; co-payments for GPs have been reduced markedly in recent years. Complementary and alternative medicines and therapies are paid for out-of-pocket. Such payments, including both cost sharing and expenditure paid directly by private households, accounted for 14 per cent of total national health expenditures in 2007.

The Government is committed to funding essential palliative care services and to ensure these are available. Healthcare public funding is derived from general taxation (85 per cent), levies on employers (7 per cent), and local government (8 per cent). Overall, public funding accounts for about 78 per cent of healthcare expenditure. However, palliative care in New Zealand is currently substantially under-resourced. The Government provides on average just over 50 per cent of hospice core functions (some hospices receive only 38 per cent of their total budget while others receive up to 75 per cent). The remaining amount is funded by public donations.

The Government spends approximately $50 million a year on palliative care, while $22 million is raised through charitable donations to fund palliative care services.

South Africa

Background

The Republic of South Africa is a multi-ethnic society five times as large as the UK, encompassing among its fifty-two million inhabitants a wide variety of cultures, languages, and religions. Its pluralistic make-up is reflected in its constitutional recognition of eleven official languages, including English, which is commonly used in public and commercial life and ranked fourth in the nation as a first-spoken language.

South Africa enjoys a relatively high GDP per capita compared to other countries in Sub-Saharan Africa ($11,750 at purchasing power parity for 2012). Despite this, South Africa is still burdened by a relatively high rate of poverty and unemployment, and is also among the top ten countries of the world for its income inequality.

Life expectancy in 2009 was 71 years for a white and 48 years for a black South African. The healthcare spending in the country is about 9 per cent of GDP. About 20 per cent of South Africa's population uses private healthcare, with 15 per cent covered by medical insurance. The rest either pay out-of-pocket (OOP) or access the subsidized care provided by the public health sector. Data from the General Household Survey 2002-2007[123] indicate that the racial distribution of medical scheme coverage is very skewed. While only ±15 per cent of the total population belongs to a medical scheme, the comparable figure is 66 per cent for the white population.[124]

People choose to purchase certain healthcare services from the private sector even if they are not insured: out of the 85 per cent of citizens who do not have medical scheme coverage, 29 per cent used a private facility and incurred OOP expenditure on healthcare while only 20 per cent did not have any OOP costs. This seems to be a reflection of people's general dissatisfaction with the public sector. User satisfaction is lower for public health facilities than it is for private ones, and this gap appears to have widened in recent years.

The Department of Health (DH) provides leadership and coordination of health services with a view to promoting the health of all people in South Africa through an accessible, caring and high quality health system based on a primary healthcare approach. This objective is not yet reached: South Africa ranks 30th among the 40 countries analyzed by the Economist Intelligent Unit in its 2010 Quality of Death survey.[125] DH is supposed to provide a framework for a structured uniform health system within South Africa. The department's goals over the medium term do not include palliative care among the strategic priorities, which feature making progress towards universal health coverage, preventing disease and promoting health, improving health facility planning by implementing norms and standards, improving financial management, developing an efficient health management information system for improved decision-making, improving the quality of care, and improving human resources for health by ensuring adequate training and accountability measures.

Palliative care services and hospice care

Palliative care is an approach that improves the quality of life of patients and their families when faced with problems associated with life-threatening illness. It promotes the prevention and relief of suffering by means of early identification, and the accurate assessment and treatment of pain and other physical, psychosocial and spiritual problems. Any person of any age who has a life-limiting condition qualifies for palliative care, provided they consent to joining a hospice programme. Many different types of illnesses are included, the most common of which are cancer and AIDS.

Hospices and partner organizations in South Africa are supported by the Hospice Palliative Care Association of South Africa (HPCA), an organization that promotes quality in life, dignity in death and support in bereavement for everyone living with a life-threatening illness.[126] The HPCA is also active in spreading the understanding that hospices are about life, living and love. This is meant to change perceptions about hospices so that people are not fearful of receiving hospice care when they or their family need it.

Hospices deliver palliative care in South Africa in three main ways:

- Hospice home-based care: mobile teams of professionally super-vised trained community caregivers travel to people's homes and support and teach families to provide care at home. Not only is this cost effective but it also allows the patient to be at home, which is often where they prefer to remain.

- Hospice community centres: many hospices work from estab-lished bases within the community. At these bases they meet with groups of people who have palliative care needs. The type of patient who would attend these meetings is still reasonably well and mobile. Doctors, nurses, social workers and other pro-fessionals will attend the centres regularly to assist those with individual needs. These centres provide excellent forums where people facing life-limiting illness can connect meaningfully with others in support groups. At many such centres, a variety of skills are also taught and income-generating projects initiated.

- Hospice inpatient units: some hospices have inpatient units. This is a facility that provides 24-hour palliative care. Usually these units have a small number of beds and specific criteria for admission. A patient who has pain that is difficult to control at home, a patient whose family needs respite, or a patient who has absolutely no support systems at home are some of those who may be admitted to an inpatient unit.

Different hospices may have slightly varying admission criteria depending on their resources and limitations, such as geographical distance or staff availability. However, all hospices are committed to seeing that patients' palliative care needs are met. Anyone may refer a patient to a hospice: friends, neighbours, family members or the patients themselves. Hospice nurses will then visit patients to assess whether they are in need of pal-liative care. Patients may also be admitted if they have a direct referral from a healthcare professional (a doctor or nurse).

When a patient is accepted into a hospice programme, the hospice team together with the patient develop a tailor-made plan of care. The main things a hospice can help with are pain and symptom control, psycho-social support and advice, spiritual and emotional support and bereavement support. The hospice may also help in equipping the patient's home with essential equipment, such as a bed, wheelchair or commode.

Palliative care in South Africa does not address only the elderly: child mortality in South Africa is high, although under-five mortality declined between 2000 and 2011, from 74 to 47 per thousand live births. The decline was attributed to the provision of better services to communities. In 2012, only 2.7 per cent of HIV positive mothers transmitted the virus to their babies, a significant decrease from previous years.

'The majority of people have seen people dying since they were children', says Irish doctor Anne Merriman, Nobel Peace Prize winner and leader of Palliative Care in Africa, 'so they're much better at bereavement than we are'. Palliative Treatment for Children South Africa (PATCH) is an inclusive and compassionate network that aims to share specialized knowledge, to provide tools and opportunities to ensure the best possible care for children with life-threatening and life-limiting illnesses, and to offer support to families and lay caregivers. PATCH membership is composed of healthcare professionals, family members and community members with an interest in palliative care for children.

Where care is provided

Unlike many Western countries, in South Africa death is not a taboo. Death, particularly since AIDS swept across the continent, is never far away. Africans also have strong community care networks through family and friends. 'If someone is living alone, the neighbours will come and help because they're part of the community', says Anne Merriman. This is reflected in the Quality of Death Index, in which South Africa scores highly when it comes to the availability of volunteer workers for end-of-life care.[127]

Aside from hospice programmes, palliative care may also be delivered by trained specialists across the healthcare continuum. Some hospitals have palliative care teams or wards. Through HPCA-driven initiatives, many doctors, nurses, pastors and social workers from NGOs and the public and private healthcare sector are receiving training in and providing palliative care.

Hospices can be found throughout the country and their number is increasing. In 2011 there were 202 hospices compared with 52 hospices in 2004.

Location and information on hospices in each province can be found at the HPCA site.[128]

Legal aspects

In the 1990s, the South African Law Commission conducted an exhaustive review of the state of the law with regard to end-of-life, concluding that: 'At present, the position in our law is that the termination of a person's life is unlawful, even if the motive for such conduct is to end the person's unbearable suffering, even where the suffering person has expressed the wish to die or has even begged to be killed.'[129] Such as it is, the law relies on portions of cognate legislation and case law. The Commission reviewed a selection of cases of mercy killing that went to trial. The perpetrators were found guilty of murder but none served an actual jail sentence. Perhaps because of community sympathy, 'the courts sought to reflect the sense of justice of the community regarding the blameworthiness of the accused by imposing very light sentences'.[130]

The euthanasia debate in South Africa essentially concerns the balance between the constitutional guarantees of the right to life, and the rights to dignity and to autonomy. The right to life 'is not merely a right to biological life; it is a claim and entitlement to a particular quality of life', wrote Daniel J. Ncayiyana, adding:

> It does not follow that South Africa is a safe and appropriate place for liberalised voluntary euthanasia legislation. Euthanasia − a recourse of last resort − can only really be justified in a country with the very best medical care for all, a well-organised and universally accessible palliative care and support system, stable and well-functioning (particularly judicial) institutions, and a strong culture of respect for human life. In South Africa, with its severe constraints on health care facilities and the totally inadequate allocation of resources for highly effective medical treatments, there is a real risk of euthanasia becoming a substitute for proper care for the terminally ill and other patients in dire medical straits.
>
> Even more damning for South Africa is the pervasive lack of an ethos of respect for human life. We are an extraordinarily violent society, with over 45 murders committed daily and interpersonal violence the second highest cause of death. Mob justice, police brutality and xenophobia abound. Needless deaths occur regularly in our hospitals through staff neglect and

indifference. Health care providers think nothing of downing tools and walking off, abandoning critically ill patients, or of blocking ambulances with critical emergencies from entering health facilities during labour disputes.

In the circumstances, euthanasia cannot be at the top of the wish-list of things that must be accomplished in order to improve the human condition of South Africans.[131]

Other relevant subjects involved in the legal debate are advance directives, terminal pain management and withholding and withdrawing potentially life-sustaining treatments.[132]

Advance directives involve an end-of-life decision-making practice that recognizes the moral right of individuals to future control over their medical treatment in the eventuality that they may become incompetent to make their own end-of-life decisions. Clear affirmation in statutory law with regard to the legal status of advance directives would assist in focusing people's minds on making decisions at the right time about possible future scenarios in which they would not want to find themselves helpless to decide. There are two main classes of advance directives:

- A 'living will' is an instruction directive by which a competent person instructs others to withhold or withdraw potentially life-sustaining treatment should they become incapable of refusing such treatment themselves.

- A 'power of attorney for healthcare' is a substitute directive by which a competent person appoints or mandates a specific person as their proxy healthcare decision-maker should they become incompetent to make their own healthcare decisions.

Appropriate and adequate terminal pain management that provides comfort and care to a patient suffering from a terminal disease and whose death is imminent may have the secondary effect of hastening death. Potentially, this exposes medical practitioners to criminal and civil liability. Consequently, there is a need for legislative clarity that ensures adequate terminal pain management according to the standard of medical care appropriate in the circumstances. This could be ensured by an honest application of the doctrine of double effect: legitimizing the possible shortening of life if that is the foreseen but unintended outcome of appropriately managing terminal pain and suffering.

Withholding and withdrawing potentially life-sustaining treatment is an end-of-life decision-making practice that recognizes the moral right to a natural death of individuals in the terminal phase of dying, as well as the corresponding moral obligation of caregivers, family and state to respect that right. The law should be clear about the legal status of this right and obligation. The law should recognize and create the space for ethically responsible decision-making with regard to withholding or withdrawing potentially life-sustaining treatment from competent and incompetent persons.

Cost of palliative care

In South Africa, hospice palliative care is given freely, regardless of a person's ability to pay.[133] South African hospices rely on funding support from government, corporations and communities. Volunteers are also essential to the work in local hospices. The South African government is moving fast to integrate palliative care into the health systems, but it is still limited by resources. This calls for creative ways of diversifying the funding.

Palliative care funding should be seen as a very useful investment for governments. The palliative care approach has contributed not only to reducing suffering among patients with cancer, AIDS and other conditions, but also programmes using the palliative care approach have demonstrated their cost effectiveness and reduced unnecessary patient admissions. In addition, AIDS programmes using the palliative care approach have contributed significantly to prevention of further HIV transmission through accessing other family members, and to tracking, testing and treating children and adults living with HIV.

The Abundant Life programme established at Victoria Hospital in Cape Town and adapted for the South African setting from the UK Gold Standards Framework, has proved successful in assisting patients with organ failure, and in reducing the number of hospital admissions for this group of patients. A report on this programme also demonstrated savings for patients and for hospitals.[134]

The palliative care fraternity in South Africa has received assistance from traditional palliative care donors such as the US government through PEPPFAR, the UK Government through DFID, and the EU through

International Cooperation and Development, as well as from trusts, foundations and other funding institutions and individuals. These entities have provided direct funding, twinning programmes and training opportunities for staff.

However, as a result of the 2009 worldwide economic crisis, donor funding has been seriously reduced, and hospices in South Africa are being forced to reduce staff and cut back on the numbers of patients they care for.

Bibliography

BIANCHI, Enzo, *Il Male, la Malattia, la Morte*, Qiqajon, Magnano 2008

BIANCHI, Enzo, *Vivere l'anzianità*, Bose, Qiqajon, Magnano 2010

CACCIARI, Massimo et al., *Morte, fine o passaggio?*, Rizzoli, Milano 2007

DESMET, Marc, *Souffrance et dignité humaine*, Fidéliyé, Namur 2004

DESMET, Marc, *Jour et nuit. Expérience médicale et spiritualité*, Lessius, Bruxelles 2006

FROMM, Erich, *To Have or to Be*, Bloomsbury, London 1976

GALIMBERTI, Umberto, *Orme del sacro*, Feltrinelli, Milano 2000

GALIMBERTI, Umberto, *Il segreto della domanda, Intorno alle cose umane e divine*, Apogeo, Milano 2008

HENNEZEL, Marie De, MONTIGNY, Johanne De, *L'amour ultime. L'accompagnement des mourants*, Hatier, Paris 1991

HENNEZEL, Marie De, *Seize the Day. How the Dying Teach Us to Live* (1995), Pan Macmillan, London 2007

HENNEZEL, Marie De, *Nous ne nous sommes pas dit au revoir*, Laffont Pocket Spiritualité, Paris 2000

HENNEZEL, Marie De, *Propositions pour une vie digne jusqu'au bout*, Éditions du Seuil, Paris 2004

HENNEZEL, Marie De, *Mourir les yeux ouverts*, Pocket, Paris 2005

HENNEZEL, Marie De, *The Art of Growing Old: Aging with Grace*, Penguin Books, London 2008

HENNEZEL, Marie De, *The Warmth of the Heart Prevents Your Body from Rusting*, Pan Macmillan, London 2008

HENNEZEL, Marie De, VERGELY, Bertrand, *Une vie pour se mettre au monde*, Carnets Nord, Paris 2010

HONORÉ, Carl, *In Praise of Slow*, Orion Books, Toronto 2004

KEOWN, John, *Euthanasia, Ethics and Public Policy. An Argument Against Legislation*, Cambridge University Press, Cambridge 2002

KÜBLER-ROSS, Elisabeth, *On Death and Dying And The Five Stages of Grief*, Routledge, Abdingdon 1969

KÜBLER-ROSS, Elisabeth, *Death the Final Stage of Growth*, A Touchstone Book, New York 1975

KÜBLER-ROSS, Elisabeth, *On Children and Death*, A Touchstone Book, New York 1983

KÜBLER-ROSS, Elisabeth, *On Life After Death*, Celestial Arts, Berkeley 1991

KÜBLER-ROSS, Elisabeth, *Death is of Vital Importance: On Life, Death and Life After Death*, Station Hill Press, New York 1995

KÜBLER-ROSS, Elisabeth, *Sterben lernen, Leben lernen*, Die Silberschnur Verlag, Güllesheim 1995

KÜBLER-ROSS, Elisabeth, *The Tunnel and the Light. Essential Insights on Living and Dying, with a Letter to a Child with Cancer*, Da Capo Press, Cambridge 1999

KÜBLER-ROSS, Elisabeth, KESSLER, David, *On Grief and Grieving*, Simon and Schuster, London 2005

MONTERO, Étienne, ARS, Bernard (sous la direction de), *Euthanasie, les enjeux du débat*, Presses de la Renaissance, Paris 2005

MONTERO, Étienne, *Rendez-vous avec la mort*, Anthemis, Limal 2013

M'UZAN, Michel de, *De l'art à la mort*, Gallimard, Paris 1983

SAUNDERS, Cicely M., *Care of the dying*, Macmillan, London 1976

SAUNDERS, Cicely M., *Watch with Me. Inspiration for a life in hospice care* (1965), Mortal Press, Sheffield 2003

SAUNDERS, Cicely M., *Beyond the Horizon. A Search for Meaning in Suffering*, Dalton, Longman and Todd, London 1990

SAUNDERS, Cicely M., *Living with Dying: A Guide to Palliative Care*, Oxford Medical Publications, Oxford 1995

SŒUR LÉONTINE (Buysscher, Josefa de), *Au nom de la vie*, Racine, Bruxelles 1992

VERONESI, Umberto, *Il diritto di non soffrire. Cure palliative, testamento biologico, eutanasia*, Mondadori, Milano 2011

VERSPIEREN, Patrick, *Face à celui qui meurt*, Deselée de Brouwer, Paris 1984

VERSPIEREN, Patrick, RICHARD, Marie-Sylvie, RICOT, Jacques, *La tentation de l'euthanasie*, Desclée de Brouwer, Paris 2004

WORLD HEALTH ORGANIZATION, *Palliative Care: Knowledge into Action. Guide for Effective Programmes*, 2007, http://www.who.int/cancer/media/FINAL-Palliative%20Care%20Module.pdf [Accessed 25/08/2014]

Notes

To help readers access the weblinks in this section, the entire notes section can be found on the author's website: http://www.stanjano.org/En/Notes.pdf

1. Marie De Hennezel, *Seize the Day, How the Dying Teach Us to Live* (1995), Pan Macmillan, London, 2007.
2. For palliative care see Appendix, p. 131.
3. Lucius Annaeus Seneca, 'Mors aut finis aut transitus in Epistole morali a Lucilio' (Dante Alighieri, Rome, 2007) n. 65, quoted by Ivano Dionigi in Massimo Cacciari et al., *Morte, fine o passaggio?*, Rizzoli, Milan, 2007, p. 9.
4. Maurice Zundel, quoted by Marie de Hennezel, *Mourir les yeux ouverts*, Albin Michel, Paris, 2005, p. 73. Marie de Hennezel, *La mort intime. Ceux qui vont mourir nous apprennent à vivre*, Laffont, Paris, 1995, p. 207.
5. Michel De M'Uzan, *De l'art à la mort*, Gallimard, Paris, 1983, pp. 182–199.
6. Hennezel, *La mort intime*, cit. p. 207.
7. Enzo Bianchi, *Vivere l'anzianità*, Bose, Edizioni Qiqajon, 2010.
8. NTBR: a medical term that stands for Not To Be Reanimated. When this is written with informed consent in the medical record of a dying patient, should cardiac arrest occur, the health care personnel do not perform emergency resuscitation treatment.
9. 'Unfinished business': all those matters we have put on hold but which should be finished before it's too late. See Elisabeth Kübler-Ross, *On Death and Dying*, Routledge, Abingdon, 1969 (40th Anniversary Edition 2009), p. 213; Marie de Hennezel, *La mort intime. Ceux qui vont mourir nous apprennent à vivre*, Laffont, 1995, pp. 55–56.
10. A 2002 Belgian law regulates euthanasia. See Appendix on page 141.
11. Umberto Veronesi, *Il diritto di non soffrire. Cure palliative, testamento biologico, eutanasia*, Mondadori, Milan, 2011, p. 99.
12. Marie de Hennezel, *Nous ne nous sommes pas dit au revoir*, Laffont, Paris, 2000, Pocket Spiritualité, pp. 223–53; Étienne Montero, 'Les enjeux socio-politiques de l'euthanasie', in Étienne Montero, Bernard Ars (Ed.), *Euthanasie, les enjeux du débat*, Presses de la Renaissance, Paris, 2005, pp. 247–73.
13. See Appendix on Belgian about the law regarding euthanasia on page 141.
14. Soeur Leontine (Buysscher, Josefa de), *Au nom de la vie*, Éditions Racine, Brussels, 1992.

15. Hennezel, *Nous nous sommes pas dit au revoir* cit., passim.
16. Ibid, p. 166.
17. Chalet Robinson is a bar and restaurant located on an island in the Bois de la Cambre in Brussels.
18. From the Gospel of Luke, 17:10 (inter-confessional translation): 'When you have done all that is commanded you, say, "We are only servants. We did what we had to do."'
19. Romano Madera, participant in the Round Table: *Define Spirituality in Practice: Philosophies in Dialogue*, XIX National Congress of the Italian Society of Palliative Care, Turin, 2012.
20. Michael Ende, *Momo, oder die seltsame Geschichte von den Zeit-Dieben und von dem Kind, das den Menschen die gestohlene Zeit zurckbracte*, K. Thienemanns Verlag, Stuttgart, 1973, p. 54.
21. Patrick Verspieren, *Face à celui qui meurt*, Desclée de Brouwer, Paris 1984, mentioned in the exhibition *Si un jour Je meurs*, Brussels, 11 March–25 April 2011, www.espacefusterie.ch/index.php/extras-fusterie/expositions/47-si-un-jour-je-meurs. [Accessed 3 March 2014].
22. The death of the individual preserves humanity; humanity filled with old men could not survive: Marie de Hennezel, Bertrand Vergely, *Une vie pour se mettre au monde*, Éditions Carnets Nord, Paris, 2010, p. 85.
23. Chantal Delvaulx, *Vivre jusqu'au bout* (Beauvechain, Éditions Nauwelaerts, 1997) p. 98.
24. See Appendix on page 138.
25. Pio Parisi, *La pietra scartata*, Easter 2001, <http://www.donvitaliano.it/vecchiosito/La%20pietra%20scartata.htm> [Accessed 24 August 2014].
26. Incontri di discernimento e solidarietà [Meetings of Discernment and Solidarity], <http://www.incontripioparisi.it/discernimento/2010-11_La_messa_sul_mondo/traccia.php> [Accessed 24 August 2014].
27. Guy Gilbert, *Face à la souffrance* (Paris, Éditions Philippe Rey, 2009), p. 78.
28. Continuing Care, Soins continus palliatifs et à domicile, http://www.continuing-care.be/ [Accessed 3 March 2015].
29. To keep the time of dying within the field of communication or to return it there: Patrick Verspieren et al., *La tentation de l'euthanasie*, Desclée Éditions de Brouwer, Paris, 2004, p. 112.
30. Umberto Galimberti, *Il segreto della domanda. Intorno alle cose umane e divine*, Apogeo, Milan, 2008, p. 71 and following.
31. Erich Fromm, *L'amore per la vita*, Mondadori, Milan, 1984, p. 27.
32. Marie de Hennezel, Johanne de Montigny, *L'amour ultime. L'accompagnement*

des mourants, Hatier, Paris 1991, p.118; Marie de Hennezel, *La mort intime. Ceux qui vont mourir nous apprennent à vivre*, Laffont, Paris, 1995, p. 16.

33. Carl Honoré, *In Praise of Slow*, Orion Books, Toronto 2004, p. 3 and passim.

34. Marc Desmet, *Jour et nuit. Expérience médicale et spiritualité*, Éditions Lessius, Brussels, 2006, pp. 169–86; *Souffrance et dignité humaine*, Éditions Fidélité, Namur, 2004, pp. 83–90. Speaking of the doctor's impotence in the face of death and his or her necessary 'passivity' in the extreme phases of the illness, Desmet notes that, in French, *passivité* sounds the same as *pas si vite* [not so fast], an invitation to respect the patient's perception of the flow of time.

35. Donatien Mallet, *Pratiques soignantes et dépénalisation de l'euthanasie*, L'Harmattan, Paris, 2012, p. 137 ff.

36. *Penser solidairement la fin de vie*, report for François Hollande, President of the French Republic, 18 December 2012 <http://www.elysee.fr/communiques-de-presse/article/rapport-de-la-commission-de-reflexion-sur-la-fin-de-vie-en-france/> [Accessed 24 August 2014].

37. Quoted by Father SJ Scholters from *Position de l'Église à l'égard de l'euthanasie*, at the conference *Éthique et fin de vie*, held 7 December 2013 at Solbosch ULB campus, Brussels.

38. Marie de Hennezel, Montigny, *L'amour ultime*, cit., p. 12.

39. Sergio Mattarella Intervento alla Presentazione del libro *L'amore, sempre* di Attilio Stajano a Palermo, Sabato 14 giugno 2014 a Villa Albanese http://www.stajano.org/LAS2/%29INTERVENTO-SM.htm [Accessed 19 April 2015].

40. Enzo Bianchi, *Vivere l'anzianità*, cit., passim.

Appendix

1. http://www.who.int/cancer/media/FINAL-Palliative%20Care%20Module.pdf [Accessed 18 July 2015].

2. David Clark, 'International progress in creating palliative medicine as a specialised discipline', in Geoffrey Hanks (Ed.) *Oxford Textbook of Palliative Medicine*, Oxford University Press, 2011.

3. Sheila Payne and Tom Lynch, 'International progress in creating palliative medicine as a specialized discipline and the development of palliative care', in Nathan Cherny et al. (Ed.'s) *Oxford Textbook of Palliative Medicine* (5th ed.) Oxford: Oxford University Press, 2015.

4. M.R. Rajagopal and Reena George, 'Providing palliative care in economically

disadvantaged countries', in Nathan Cherny et al. (Ed.'s) *Oxford Textbook of Palliative Medicine* (5th ed.), cit.

5. *The quality of death: ranking end-of-life care across the world.* Economist Intelligence Unit, London; 2010. www.qualityofdeath.org [Accessed 2 June 2015].

6. John J Bonica, *The Management of Pain: With Special Emphasis on the Use of Analgesic Block in Diagnosis, Prognosis and Therapy* (London: Henry Kimpton, 1953).

7. The first hospices were opened over a century ago in Dublin (Our Lady's Hospice, 1879) and in the East End of London (St Joseph's Hospice, Hackney, 1905) by Catholic nuns as a charitable and religious mission caring for those dying of tuberculosis and living in poverty. Considerably later, St Christopher's Hospice opened in South London in 1967.

8. Mary Baines, 'From pioneer days to implementation: lessons to be learnt', *European Journal of Palliative Care*, 18, 5 (2011).

9. Thomas J. Smith and J. Brian Cassel, 'The economic challenges of palliative medicine', in Nathan Cherny et al. (Ed.'s), *Oxford Textbook of Palliative Medicine*, cit.

10. Ethics Task Force of the European Association for Palliative Care, 'Euthanasia and physician-assisted suicide: a view from an EAPC Ethics Task Force', Palliative Medicine, 2003.

11. Non-voluntary euthanasia is defined as an act conducted where the consent of the patient is unavailable. Involuntary euthanasia is defined as an act conducted against the will of the patient. Passive euthanasia is defined as an act that entails the withholding of treatment.

12. In The Netherlands, the penal code was changed, whereas in Belgium and Luxembourg it was not, and thus in these latter countries euthanasia remains voluntary premeditated homicide, punishable by penal law, and non-punishable solely under the conditions specified by the law.

13. See details in the section on the US at page 159.

14. An overview (current as of 3 September, 2015) of the current status of legislation and legislative proposals in each US state is presented by the Death with Dignity National Center at http://www.deathwithdignity.org/advocates/national [Accessed 20 September 2015].

15. See details in the section on Canada at page 165.

16. See details in the section on Australia at page 177.

17. There is one exception in the Northern Territory, Australia, as described in a following section, on page 178.

18. J. Pereira, 'Legalizing euthanasia or assisted suicide: the illusion of safeguards and controls', *Current Oncology*, 18, 2: (April 2011), pp. 38–45.

19. *The quality of death*, Economist Intelligence Unit, cit.

20. Law no. 38/2010: 'Provisions to guarantee access to palliative care and pain therapy', http://www.normattiva.it/uri-res/N2Ls?urn:nir:stato:legge:2010;38 [Accessed 24 August 2014].

21. Repubblica italiana, Ministero della Salute, *Hospice in Italia 2010, Seconda rilevazione ufficiale*, ed. by Furio Zucco, Bononia University Press, Bologna 2010.

22. Law no. 38/2010: 'Urgent Implementation of the National Health Plan 1998–2000', http://www.normattiva.it/uri-res/N2Ls?urn:nir:stato:legge:1999-02-26;39 [Accessed 24 August 2014]. Law converting the Decree of 28 December 1998 # 450 'Provisions to ensure urgent implementation of the National Health Plan 1998–2000'. <http://www.fedcp.org/pdf_normative/DECRETO_28_dicembre_1998.pdf> [Accessed 08 August 2014].

23. Ministero della salute, *Rapporto 2015 al Parlamento sullo stato di attuazione della Legge n. 38*.

24. http://www.salute.gov.it [Accessed 24 August 2014].

25. Società Italiana di Cure Palliative <http://www.sicp.it/> [Accessed 24 August 2014].

26. Text published in *Moniteur belge* (the official Belgian gazette), http://www.ejustice.just.fgov.be/cgi_loi/change_lg.pl?language=fr&la=F&table_name=loi&cn =2002052837 [Accessed 24 August 2014].

27. Text published in *Moniteur belge*, http://www.ejustice.just.fgov.be/cgi_loi/change_Ig.pl?language=fr&la=F&cn=2002061446&table_name=loi [Accessed 24 August 2014].

28. Text published in *Moniteur belge*, http://www.ejustice.just.fgov.be/cgi_loi/change_lg.pl?language=fr&la=F&table_name=loi&cn=2002082245 [Accessed 24 August 2014].

29. Law modifying the law of 28 May 2012 regarding euthanasia, extending euthanasia to include minors. Text published in *Moniteur belge*, http://www.icb-cib.org/fr/pd f/20140228-loi-cu euthanasia-mineurs.pdf [Accessed 24 August 2014].

30. Étienne Montero, *Rendez-vous avec la mort*, Anthemis, Limal, 2013, p. 33.

31. Ibidem.

32. Dominique Lossignol, 'Soins palliatifs et euthansie: la fin d'un conflit?', *La Revue des soins palliatifs en Wallonie*, n. 14, 2012, p. 24.

33. Montero, *Rendez-vous avec la mort*, cit., p. 10.

34. Paul Vanden Berghe et al., 'Assisted dying. The current situation in Flanders: euthanasia embedded in palliative care', *European Journal of Palliative Care*, vol. 20, 6 (2012), pp. 266–272.

35. Montero, *Rendez-vous avec la mort*, cit. p. 96.

36. Corinne Van Oost, *Médecin catholique, pourquoi je pratique l'euthanasie*, Paris: Presses De La Renaissance, 2014.

37. Law no. 2005-370, 22 April 2005 relating to the rights of the sick and the end of life http://www.legifrance.gouv.fr/affichTexte.do?cidTexte=JORFTEXT000000446240&dateTexte=&categorieLien=id [Accessed 24 August 2014].

38. Law no. 99-477, 9 June 1999, designed to guarantee the right of access to palliative care http://www.legifrance.gouv.fr/affichTexte.do?cidTexte=JORFTEX1UXOXl212121 [Accessed 24 August 2014].

39. Law no. 2002-303, 4 March 2002, relating to the rights of the sick and the quality of the health service http://www.legifrance.gouv.fr/affichTexte.do?cidTexte=JORFTEXT000000227015 [Accessed 24 August 2014].

40. Cécile B. Loupan, *Vivre et mourir comme un homme*, Paris: L'Œuvre, 2010.

41. *Penser solidairement la fin de vie*, A report to François Hollande, President of the French Republic, 18 December 2012, http: //www.elysee.fr/communiques-de-presse/article/rapport-de-la-commission-de-reflexion-sur-la-fin-de-vie-en-france/ [Accessed 24 August 2014].

42. Le Monde. 17.03.2015 http://www.gouvernement.fr/argumentaire/fin-de-vie [Accessed 4 August 2015].
Text of the law http://www.elysee.fr/assets/Uploads/Rapport-et-proposition-de-loi-creant-de-nouveaux-droits-en-faveur-des-malades-et-des-personnes-en-fin-de-vie.pdf [Accessed 4 August 2015].

43. http://www.senat.fr/espace_presse/actualites/201504/fin_de_vie_creer_de_nouveaux_droits_en_faveur_des_malades.html [Accessed 8 August 2015].

44. Société Française d'accompagnement et de soins palliatifs, *Histoire des soins palliatifs* http://www.sfap.org/content/histoire-des-soins-palliatifs [Accessed 24 August 2014].

45. 'Allocated beds' is the term used in French hospitals for the beds assigned to palliative care.

46. *The quality of death*, Economist Intelligence Unit, cit.

47. European Parliament, Policy Department Economic and Scientific Policy, 'Palliative Care in the European Union' PE 404.899 (2007).

48. *End of Life Care Strategy*, https://www.gov.uk/government/uploads/system/ uploads/attachment_data/file/136443/EOLC_exec_summ.pdf> [Accessed 24 August 2014].

49. A hospice is a specialist unit run by a team of doctors, nurses, social workers, counsellors and trained volunteers.

50. *Funding the Right Care and Support for Everyone. Creating a Fair and Transparent Funding System; the final report of the palliative care funding review.* An independent review for the Secretary of State for Health (2011) https:// www.gov.uk/government/uploads/system/uploads/attachment_data/file/ 215107/dh_133105.pdf [Accessed 24 August 2014].

51. David Clark, *International progress in creating palliative medicine as a specialized discipline*, cit.

52. The Association for Palliative Medicine of Great Britain and Ireland (APM) http://apmonline.org/ [Accessed 24 June 2015] is an association for doctors and medical students working in or interested in specialist palliative care, whether in hospices, hospitals or the community. Formed in 1986, it now has approximately 1000 members.

53. *Palliative Medicine*, http://pmj.sagepub.com/ [Accessed 24 June 2015] is a highly ranked, peer reviewed scholarly journal dedicated to improving knowledge and clinical practice in the palliative care of patients with far advanced disease. This outstanding journal features editorials, original papers, review articles, case reports, correspondence and book reviews.

54. C. Centeno et al., *EAPC Atlas of Palliative Care in Europe 2013 – Full Edition* (Milan: European Association for Palliative Care, 2013).

55. http://www.nhs.uk/choiceintheNHS/Rightsandpledges/NHSConstitution/ Pages/Overview.aspx [Accessed 24 June 2015].

56. General Medical Council, http://www.gmc-uk.org/guidance/ ethical_guidance/end_of_life_legal_annex.asp#3 [Accessed 24 June 2015].

57. Assisted Dying Bill (HL Bill 6), http://www.publications.parliament.uk/pa/ bills/lbill/2014-2015/0006/lbill_2014-20150006_en_2.htm#llg1 [Accessed 24 June 2015].

58. *The Guardian*, 'Assisted dying bill held up in the House of Lords', 17 January 2015.

59. *The Guardian*, 'Assisted dying bill overwhelmingly rejected by MPs', 12 September 2015.

60. Carolyn Johnston, Jane Liddle, 'The Mental Capacity Act 2005: a new framework for healthcare decision-making', *Journal of Medical Ethics* 33, 2, pp. 94–97.

61. NHS continuing healthcare, http://www.nhs.uk/Planners/end-of-life-care/Pages/nhs-continuing-healthcare.aspx [Accessed 24 June 2015].

62. C. Centeno et al., *EAPC Atlas of Palliative Care in Europe*, 2013 http://hdl.handle.net/10171/29291 [Accessed 24 June 2015]; *Palliative care for older people: better practices*, ed. by Sue Hall et al., World Health Organization WHO Regional Office for Europe 2010.

63. Final Report of the *Palliative Care Funding Review*, An independent review for the Secretary of State for Health July 2011 <https://www.gov.uk/government/uploads/system/uploads/attachment_data/file/215107/dh_133105.pdf> [Accessed 24 June 2015].

64. Further details of the grants fund can be viewed at <http://www.dh.gov.uk/health/2012/05/hospicefunding> [Accessed 24 June 2015].

65. Melanie H. Wilson Silver, 'Patients' Rights in England and the United States of America: The Patient's Charter and the New Jersey Patient Bill of Rights: A Comparison', *Journal of Medical Ethics*, 1997, 23, pp. 213–220.

66. Sheila Payne and Tom Lynch. International progress in creating palliative medicine as a specialized discipline in Nathan Cherny et al. (Ed.'s), *Oxford Textbook of Palliative Medicine*, cit.

67. National Institute of Nursing Research, National Institute of Health, Palliative Care: *Improving quality of life when you're seriously ill*. NIH publication #11-6415 (2011).

68. NHPCO's *Facts and Figures 2013*, Hospice Care in America, NHPCO 2013.

69. http:// www.getpalliativecare.org [Accessed 17 July 2015].

70. NHPCO's *Facts and Figures*, cit.

71. Diane E Meier, 'Increased Access to Palliative Care and Hospice Services: Opportunities to Improve Value in Healthcare', *Milbank Quarterly*, September 2011, 89, 3, pp. 343–380.

72. David Clark, 'From margins to centre: a review of the history of palliative care in cancer', *The Lancet Oncology*, May 2007 8, 5, pp. 430–438.

73. Diane E Meier, *Increased Access to Palliative Care*, cit.

74. <http://www.nhs.uk/choiceintheNHS/Rightsandpledges/NHSConstitution/Pages/Overview.aspx> [Accessed 2 August 2015].

75. 'A Patient's Bill of Rights', American Hospital Association 1973, revised 1992. http://www.carroll.edu/msmillie/bioethics/patbillofrights.htm [Accessed 2 August 2015].

76. The bill, A-1843, NJSA 26:2H-12.10 was passed in April 1988.

77. Melanie H. Wilson Silver, 'Patients' Rights in England and the United States of America: "The Patient's Charter" and the New Jersey Patient Bill of Rights: A Comparison', *Journal of Medical Ethics* Vol. 23, No. 4 (Aug., 1997), pp. 213–220.

78. Associated Press, 'Assisted-Suicide Bill Approved by California Lawmakers', 11 Sept 2015. http://www.nbcnews.com/news/us-news/assisted-suicide-bill-approved-california-lawmakers-n426156

79. An overview (current as of 3 September 2015) of the status of legislation and legislative proposals about end of life regulation in each US state is presented by the Death with Dignity National Center http://www.deathwithdignity.org/advocates/national [Accessed 20 September 2015].

80. E. J. Emanuel, 'The History of Euthanasia Debates in the United States and Britain', *Annals of Internal Medicine*, 1994 121, 10, pp. 793–802.

81. E. J. Emanuel, *The Ends of Human Life: Medical Ethics in a Liberal Polity*, Cambridge, MA: Harvard University Press, 1991.

82. Elisabeth Kübler-Ross, *On Death and Dying And The Five Stages of Grief*, Abingdon: Routledge, 1969. See also note 9 on p. 197.

83. Medicare hospice benefits <https://www.medicare.gov/Pubs/pdf/02154.pdf> [Accessed 23 September 2015].

84. Medicaid hospice benefits <http://www.medicaid.gov/medicaid-chip-program-information/by-topics/benefits/hospice-benefits.html> [Accessed 23 September 2015].

85. Health Maintenance Organization (HMO) <https://www.healthcare.gov/glossary/health-maintenance-organization-HMO/> [Accessed 23 September 2015].

86. Palliative Care Costs and Benefits <http://www.caringinfo.org/i4a/pages/index.cfm?pageid=3297> [accessed 24 June 2015].

87. Julie Appleby, 'Debate surrounds end-of-life healthcare costs', *USA Today*, July 10–11, 2011.

88. Philippe Couillard Minister of Health and Social Services, *Quebec End- of-Life Palliative Care Policy* http://www.chpca.net/media/7856/Quebec_policy.pdf [Accessed 24 July 2015].

89. David C. Currow and Stein Kaasa, 'Policy in palliative care', in Nathan Cherny et al. (Ed.'s) *Oxford Textbook of Palliative Medicine* (5th ed.), cit.

90. Francis J. Turner, *Encyclopedia Of Canadian Social Work* (Wilfrid Laurier University Press, 2005).

91. Robert Fowler, Departments of Medicine and Critical Care Medicine, Sunnybrook Hospital, Toronto, Ontario, Canada, *End-of-Life Care in Canada* (Clin Invest Med 2013), 36 (3), pp. 127–132.

92. Philippe Couillard, *Quebec End- of-Life Palliative Care Policy*, cit.

93. Canadian Directory of Hospice Palliative Care Services

http://www.chpca.net/family-caregivers/directory-of-services.aspx [Accessed 11 August 2015].

94. <http://hospicecare.com/home> [Accessed 11 August 2015].

95. *Carter v. Canada (Attorney General)*, 2015 SCC 5 http://scc-csc.lexum.com/ scc-csc/scc-csc/en/item/14637/index.do [Accessed 18 July 2015].

96. 'An Act respecting end-of-life care', http://www.assnat.qc.ca/en/ travaux-parlementaires/projets-loi/projet-loi-52-41-1.html [Accessed 18 July 2015].

97. Corinne Hodgson, *Cost-effectiveness of Palliative Care*, Canadian Hospice Palliative Care Association, The Way Forward Integration Initiative <http:// www.hpcintegration.ca> [Accessed 18 July 2015].

98. Yu M., Guerriere D.N., Coyte P.C., *Societal costs of home and hospital end-of-life care for palliative care patients in Ontario, Canada*, Health Soc Care Community, 2 December 2014. doi: 10.1111/hsc.12170. [Accessed 18 July 2015].

99. Tom Blackwell, 'Last month of life costs health-care system', *National Post*, 7 April 2015.

100. <http://www.cancer.ie> [Accessed 27 August 2015].

101. 'Majority believe assisted suicide should be legal', *The Irish Times*, 17 September 2010.

102. *Citizens' Information* <http://www.citizensinformation.ie/en/health/ legal_matters_and_health/advance_care_directives.html> [Accessed 27 August 2015].

103. Colm Harmon and Brian Nolan, 'Health insurance and health services utilization in Ireland', *Health Economics*, 10, 2 (March 2001), 135–145.

104. St Francis Hospice's *Annual Report*, 2010.

105. <https://www.galwayhospice.ie/> [Accessed 27 August 2015].

106. Australian Institute of Health and Welfare, 'Rural, regional and remote health: Indicators of health status and determinants of health', (March 2008), *Rural Health Series* no. 9. Cat. no. PHE 97. Canberra: ISSN 1448 9775; ISBN 978 1 74024 768 9.

107. Andrew Taylor and Margaret Box, 'Multicultural Palliative Care Guidelines', *Palliative Care Australia*, 1999. ISBN: 0-646-38432-5.

108. 'Supporting Australians to Live Well at the End of Life. National Palliative Care Strategy 2010', endorsed by Australian Health Ministers, ISBN: 978-1-74241-367-9.

109. Ibidem.

110. *The quality of death*. Economist Intelligence Unit, cit.

111. Beverley McNamara, 'Good enough death: autonomy and choice in Australian palliative care', *Social Science & Medicine*, 58, 5, (March 2004), 929–938.

112. The telephone number and the URL of local state or territory palliative care member organisation is as follows:
    NSW – 02 9206 2094 http://palliativecarensw.org.au/site/
    QLD – 1800 660 055 http://palliativecareqld.org.au/
    VIC – 03 9662 9644 http://www.pallcarevic.asn.au/
    ACT – 02 6273 9606 http://www.pallcareact.org.au/
    NT – 08 8951 6762 http://www.nt.palliativecare.org.au/
    WA – 1300 551 704 http://palliativecarewa.asn.au/site/
    SA – 08 8271 1643 http://www.pallcare.asn.au/
    TAS – 03 6231 2799 http://www.tas.palliativecare.org.au/

113. John Keown, *Euthanasia, Ethics and Public Policy: An Argument against Legislation* (Cambridge University Press, 2002).

114. Australian Government Common Law, *Euthanasia Laws Act 1997*, https://www.comlaw.gov.au/Details/C2004A05118 [Accessed 17 Sept 2015].

115. David W Kissane et al. 'Seven Deaths in Darwin: Case Studies under the Rights of the Terminally Ill Act, Northern Territories, Australia' (1998), 352 *Lancet* 1097.

116. Queensland Health Ethics Team Clinical Policy Unit Centre for Healthcare Improvement, *Implementation Guidelines: End-of-life care: Decision-making for withholding and withdrawing life sustaining measures from adult patients*, <https://www.health.qld.gov.au/qhpolicy/docs/gdl/qh-gdl-005-1-2.pdf> [Accessed 29 August 2015].

117. *The quality of death*, Economist Intelligence Unit, cit.

118. *The New Zealand Palliative Care Strategy 2001*, New Zealand Ministry of Health, ISBN 0-478-24310-3.

119. Michael McCabe, 'The Hospice Movement in New Zealand: 25 Years On', *The Nathaniel Centre* (The New Zealand Catholic Bioethics Centre), Issue 13, (August 2004).

120. Hospice New Zealand <http://www.hospice.org.nz/> [Accessed 25 August 2015].

121. The URL of each Hospice is *http://hospicecare.com/global-directory-of-providers-organizations/listings/details*, followed by the listing number in the third column below. For example, the Kaipara Palliative Care Society at Dargaville is <http://hospicecare.com/global-directory-of-providers-organizations/listings/details/254/>.

Amitabha Hospice Service	Forrest Hill, Auckland	/243/
Arohanui Hospice Service	Palmerston North	/244/
Ashburton Palliative Care	Ashburton	/245/
Community Hospice Service	Whakatane	/247/
Cranford Hospice	Hastings	/248/
Hibiscus Coast Hospice	Whangaparaoa	/250/
Hospice Bay of Islands	Kerikeri	/252/
Hospice New Zealand	Wellington	/210/
Hospice Wanganui	Wanganui	/253/
Kaipara Palliative Care Society	Dargaville	/254/

122. Hospice New Zealand, cit.
123. R. Burger and S. Van der Berg, 'How well is the South African public health care system serving its people? Transformation Audit: Risk and Opportunity', *Cape Town: Institute of Justice and Reconciliation*, 2008.
124. 'What does the demand for healthcare look like in SA?', *Econex*, NHI Note 3, October 2009. <http://www.mediclinic.co.za/about/Documents/ECONEX%20NHInote%203.pdf> [Accessed 4 September 2015].
125. *The quality of death*, Economist Intelligence Unit, cit.
126. HPCA Hospice Palliative Care of South Africa <http://www.hpca.co.za/Hospice/vision-mission.html> [Accessed 2 September 2015].
127. *The quality of death*, Economist Intelligence Unit, cit.
128. Location and information on Hospices in each province is found at the following URLs:

Eastern Cape	http://www.hpca.co.za/category/eastern-cape.html
Free State	http://www.hpca.co.za/category/free-state.html
Gauteng	http://www.hpca.co.za/category/gauteng.html
Kwa Zulu Natal	http://www.hpca.co.za/category/kwa-zulu-natal.html
Limpopo	http://www.hpca.co.za/category/limpopo.html
Mpumalanga	http://www.hpca.co.za/category/mpumalanga.html
Northern Cape	http://www.hpca.co.za/category/northern-cape.html
North West Province	http://www.hpca.co.za/category/north-west-province.html

129. Daniel J. Ncayiyana, Euthanasia – no dignity in death in the absence of an ethos of respect for human life', *The South African Medical Journal*, 102, 6 (2012).
130. Ibidem.
131. Ibidem.

132. Willem A Landman, *End-of-life-decisions, ethics and law: A case for statutory legal clarity and reform in South Africa*, Ethics Institute of South Africa, Hatfield, 2012 <www.ethicssa.org> [Accessed 20 July 2015].

133. Liz Gwyther, 'Compassion is what counts', Hospice Palliative Care Association Conference SA, 2014.

134. Liz Gwyther, 'Palliative care in chronic disease', *South African Medical Journal*, 104, 2, Cape Town (Feb. 2014).